We Love
QUINOA

The Taunton Press
Inspiration for hands-on living®

The Taunton Press, Inc. 63 South Main Street,
PO Box 5506, Newtown, CT 06470-5506
email: tp@taunton.com

This book was designed, conceived, and produced by
Quantum Books Ltd.
6 Blundell Street
London N7 9BH
United Kingdom

Publisher: Kerry Enzor
Project Editors: Charlotte Frost and Lucy Kingett
Editorial Assistant: Emma Harverson
Production Manager: Zarni Win
Designer: Simon Goggin
Photography by Simon Pask

Library of Congress Cataloging-in-Publication Data

Burns-Booth, Karen S., author.
We love quinoa : fresh and healthy inspiring recipes /
Karen S. Burns-Booth, Carolyn Cope, Jassy Davis, Kristina
Sloggett, Jackie Sobon.
pages cm
ISBN 978-1-63186-361-5
1. Cooking (Quinoa) I. Title.
TX809.Q55B43 2016
641.6'56--dc23
2015034211

Manufactured in China by
Shanghai Offset Printing Products Ltd.
10 9 8 7 6 5 4 3 2 1

We Love QUINOA

FRESH AND HEALTHY INSPIRING RECIPES

Karen S. Burns-Booth
Carolyn Cope
Jassy Davis
Kristina Sloggett
Jackie Sobon

The Taunton Press

CONTENTS

22,24,32,36,48,51,58,66,78

KEY TO SYMBOLS

Ⓥ **VEGETARIAN**

🆅🅶 **VEGAN (AND VEGETARIAN)**

🅳🅵 **DAIRY-FREE**

🅶🅵 **GLUTEN-FREE**

🆆🅵 **WHEAT-FREE**

Vegetarian and vegan recipes are tagged at the top of the pages showing main recipes.

MEET THE BLOGGERS

KAREN S. BURNS-BOOTH is a professional recipe writer and food stylist who splits her time between the U.K. and France. In addition to writing for her own site, **Lavender and Lovage**, she regularly contributes to a variety of print publications and creates recipes for major brands in the U.K. and Europe.

CAROLYN COPE is a food and lifestyle writer and the voice behind the popular blog **Umami Girl**, where the world is equal parts eat-to-live and live-to-eat. An avid traveler, musician, and yogi, she is based in greater New York City.

JASSY DAVIS is a London-based recipe writer for British organic vegetable company Abel & Cole and a professional food stylist. Her recipes in this book are inspired by Asian flavors and world food. Her blog is **Gin and Crumpets**.

KRISTINA SLOGGETT is a vegan health-food writer and recipe developer. Her blog **spabettie** focuses on plant-based recipes with vibrant colors and bright flavors for the vegan community. She currently lives in Portland, Oregon.

JACKIE SOBON is both the chef and the photographer behind the blog **Vegan Yack Attack**; cooking food and taking beautiful pictures is her passion and "Camera Eats First" is her motto. Her work has been featured on websites, on news outlets, and in magazines around the globe.

WHY WE LOVE QUINOA

QUINOA (PRONOUNCED "KEEN-WAH") IS A FANTASTIC "SUPER" FOOD THAT IS COMPATIBLE WITH GLUTEN-FREE, VEGAN, AND VEGETARIAN DIETS.

QUINOA IS ANCIENT

Quinoa has been feeding humans for thousands of years. People in the Andean region of South America—Peru, Bolivia, Ecuador, Chile, and Colombia—first began domesticating the crop between 3,000 and 4,000 years ago. All crops change over time, but thanks to the maintenance of nature-friendly ancestral farming practices by the people of the Andes, quinoa continues to exist in its natural state. That's great news from both a global health perspective and a culinary one, because quinoa offers a mild but unique flavor profile that cooks are lucky to have. Quinoa is being touted as a reliable contribution to global food security. It's a high-quality food source that thrives in challenging climates, and it has the potential to help feed the world's growing population in years to come. On this basis, the United Nations even designated 2013 the international year of quinoa.

IN THE KITCHEN

Quinoa is often included in discussions about whole grains because it shares a lot of their culinary properties and proclivities. Technically, though, it's a pseudo-grain—an edible seed related to spinach, beets, and amaranth.

Quinoa grows in a rainbow of colors, but by far the most common varieties are white, red, and black. You can use them interchangeably, especially if it's difficult to find the variety called for in a recipe. Here's what you need to know about each color: White quinoa cooks up a little softer than the other varieties, making it especially great for porridges, risotto- and paella-style dishes, and baked goods; red and black quinoa stay a little crunchier, and the individual seeds remain more separate when cooked, so they're nice in salads, mixed with whole grains for textural variety, or anywhere you'd like to advertise quinoa's presence.

Due to its impressive versatility, quinoa is a great contribution to both savory and sweet dishes, from breakfast to dessert with snacks in between. As you'll see from the recipes, quinoa also integrates well into dishes with a wide variety of

Quinoa comes in a range of different colors. The most commonly sold are red, black and white, which can be bought separately but are also sold as a tricolor mix (pictured here).

cultural origins. Though initially cultivated only in the Americas, quinoa has spread across the globe, in part because cooks the world over understand its potential to enliven traditional dishes. As well as cooking the quinoa you can also puff it (see page 66), sprout it (see page 91) or use it in its flour form.

Quinoa flour is a flavorful and versatile ingredient that can be used to replace wheat flour in a range of baked goods and other recipes. It is increasingly available in stores as well as being easy to make at home.

To make quinoa flour, rinse the grains and then toast them until they are completely dry. Place the toasted quinoa into a high-speed blender or a spice grinder and process it until finely ground.

Try substituting all-purpose flour with quinoa flour in pancake recipes; using a spoonful to thicken a soup or stew; or adding a scoop to a smoothie for an extra dose of protein and fiber.

QUINOA IS GOOD FOR YOU

Quinoa's tiny size and mild taste belie its status as a nutritional powerhouse. It is a rare, plant-based source of complete protein, meaning it contains all nine of the amino acids that our bodies need but cannot produce on their own. That's why you'll often hear quinoa referred to as a high-quality protein source.

In addition to protein, quinoa boasts a substantial amount of dietary fiber; lots of antioxidants; plenty of iron, potassium, magnesium; and vitamins B, K, and E. And that's just what we know today. Since quinoa is a whole food with ancient roots, it's safe to assume that its benefits far outpace our current nutritional understanding. We can simply eat it and reap more advantages than we know.

And if that isn't enough, quinoa is also gluten-free. Because it can mimic ingredients such as flour, breadcrumbs, and grains in many recipes, quinoa is a great gift to those with gluten allergies and intolerance to wheat and other processed grains.

WHERE OUR QUINOA COMES FROM

Unlike many popular food sources today, quinoa is still grown predominantly by small farmers and associations. For that reason, and because it provides a high-quality alternative to less-efficient forms of protein derived from meat and fish, its proliferation tends to be a good thing for the environment.

Quinoa thrives in cool, arid climates where many other crops can't live. Today, the majority of quinoa still comes from the mountains and coastal valleys of Peru, Ecuador, Chile, and Bolivia. But as its popularity and profit potential increase, cultivation has spread to many parts of the world. You'll now find quinoa growing across Europe—from the Netherlands to the U.K. to Italy. In the U.S.A., quinoa grows in Colorado and Nevada, and in Canada you'll find it in Ontario.

Showing its potential to feed people across the globe, quinoa has also been grown successfully in parts of Kenya and in the Himalayas. This chart shows areas of blue where quinoa is commonly grown.

5 GREAT FLAVOR COMBINATIONS

Quinoa's adaptable flavor profile works well with a vast range of ingredient combinations. Here are five groups of complementary flavors to spark your creativity while standing in the kitchen, quinoa in hand.

- Quinoa + Garlic + Shrimp + Feta Cheese + Dill
- Quinoa + Strawberries + Swiss Chard + Pistachios + Mint
- Quinoa + Almond Milk + Cinnamon + Nutmeg + Maple Syrup
- Quinoa + Shiitake Mushrooms + Shallots + White Wine + Soy Sauce
- Quinoa + Tomatoes + Cucumber + Yellow Bell Peppers + Red Onion

10 WAYS TO EAT MORE QUINOA

1 MORNINGS

Supercharge your mornings by adding quinoa. What better way to start the day? Toast some quinoa for added crunch in your granola, as with the Vanilla Cardamom Quinoa Granola on page 32. Or, for a creamy and nourishing start to the day, give your porridge a makeover by trying the Pecan Quinoa Porridge on page 28.

2 EGG DISHES

Give your egg dishes an extra protein boost with a generous helping of quinoa, as with the Quinoa, Cheddar, and Chive Mini Frittatas on page 48. The extra fiber and protein will help you get through busy days.

3 SALADS

Are you tired of predictable salads? Spruce them up by adding quinoa, and you'll see exactly how versatile the ancient grain is. Make the most of summer with a sweet-and-savory fix, as in the Summer Quinoa Salad with Grapefruit and Tahini Dressing on page 128. Or try the sensational Thai-Style Crab, Pomelo, and Quinoa Salad on page 136.

4 SPORTS PREP/RECOVERY

Fuel your body before or after a workout with quinoa's rich proteins and complex carbohydrates. Feel better prepared and recover more quickly with the added nutrients and tasty crunch of quinoa. You can't beat portable snacks, like the Quinoa Cinnamon Power Bites on page 154.

5 BURGERS (MEAT OR VEGGIE)

For a healthy and delicious crowd-pleaser, why not mix a generous scoop of cooked quinoa into your burger patties? Enjoy the added fiber and lighter texture, like the Quinoa Bean Burger and Basil Aïoli on page 92.

6 INSTEAD OF RICE

Discover the versatility of quinoa when you swap rice with quinoa in your favorite globally inspired dishes. Stay full and nourished for longer with the Risotto-Style Quinoa with Caramelized Onions and Mushrooms on page 106. Or use quinoa in ways you'd never considered before, as with the Sprouted Quinoa and Salmon Temaki Sushi on page 89.

7 SOUPS AND STEWS

This is one of the easiest ways to include more quinoa in your diet. Swap potatoes or noodles with quinoa to make a smart and satisfying addition to hearty soups and stews. Toss in a handful of rinsed, drained quinoa to vegetable soups, like the Roasted Cauliflower Quinoa Soup on page 118. Quinoa dumplings make a great winter warmer, as with the Spicy Peanut Veggie Stew with Quinoa Dumplings on page 96.

8 BREADING: FISH, MEAT & VEG

Breading baked meats, fish, and vegetables in quinoa can quickly turn a "tasty" dinner into a "tasty and healthy" dinner. Give comfort foods a crispy and delicious coating, as with the Quinoa-Coated Fish Stick Sandwich on page 74.

9 CAKES AND COOKIES

Let go of the guilt over satisfying your sweet tooth with the protein-rich goodness of quinoa. Enjoy something sweet and filling with extra vitamins, like the Rich and Fudgy Chocolate Brownies on page 152. Or, for a one-stop boost of energy and nutrients, add quinoa to your favorite cookies, as with the Power Boost Snickerdoodles on page 146.

10 MILKSHAKES AND BABY FOOD

Quinoa can be enjoyed by the whole family! Soft, small, and an uncommon allergen, quinoa is considered a good choice among early solid foods for your baby. Enliven creamy milkshakes, purées, and cereals with the added vitamins and fiber of quinoa. Please consult with your pediatrician first to determine what is best for your baby.

Quinoa is incredibly versatile and can be used in sweet and savory dishes alike. It works wonderfully well as a substitute for rice and noodles. Try the recipe for Veggie and Quinoa Summer Rolls with Cajun Tahini Sauce on page 76.

COOKING QUINOA IS EASY!

Cooking quinoa is easy—in many ways it's a very similar process to cooking rice. Depending on the method, you can get a creamy consistency or fluffy, dry grains.

RINSE AND REPEAT: If you've ever tried quinoa and not liked the taste, it's probably because it wasn't rinsed properly. The first step in preparing quinoa is an important one: Place it in a fine-mesh strainer and rinse it very well under lukewarm water. Continue until the water runs clear, moving the quinoa around in the strainer with your hand. Then rinse a little more. This washes away quinoa's natural coating, called saponin, which protects it from predators as it grows, but needs to be removed before cooking. Some packaged quinoa has been prerinsed, but it's best to rinse it at home anyway just to be sure.

TOAST IF YOU LIKE: Quinoa has a fairly mild flavor profile, which makes it highly versatile. But in certain dishes you'll want to bring out its full potential for nuttiness. That's when you'll take the additional step of toasting rinsed and drained quinoa in a dry pot, or in a tablespoon of oil or butter, before adding cooking liquid. Place the pan over medium-high heat, pour in the quinoa, and cook, stirring frequently, until the quinoa is dry, smells toasty, and begins to take on a hint of color. Then proceed with the recipe.

SIMMER AWAY: A good rule of thumb for the proper amount of cooking liquid is two parts liquid to one part quinoa. A particular recipe may vary this ratio slightly—a bit less for a salad, a bit more for a porridge. But if you're freewheeling in the kitchen and you stick to this ratio, the results will never be too far from perfect. Quinoa happily takes on the

FREEZING QUINOA

Even though quinoa is quick to prepare from scratch, some days you just don't have the time. That's when it's wonderful to be able to reach into the freezer for an individual portion of cooked quinoa that, once defrosted, will be virtually indistinguishable from the fresh stuff.

When you're making a pot of quinoa, double or triple the recipe. Let the leftovers cool completely. (You can speed this process by spreading it out on a rimmed cookie sheet if you like.) Then measure out individual portions—a cup or two works nicely—and place into zip-top bags or small, lidded containers. For reference, a sandwich bag holds about two cups (360 g).

Squeeze any air out of the bags and place in the freezer, inside a larger freezer-safe bag if you like. Freeze for up to 3 months. When ready to use, simply defrost on the counter or place in a bowl in the microwave for about a minute.

flavors of the liquid in which it's cooked, and there's virtually no limit to the options you can try. Water works just fine in most cases. Swirl in a little fine sea salt and a knob of butter or drizzle of oil if you like. Or feel free to get fancy. A richly flavored stock will shine in a savory dish. Dairy and nondairy milks add creaminess to porridge, while juices like apple and orange brighten up sweet salads and desserts. Add a splash of wine when it feels right, and experiment freely with mixing liquids.

With your quinoa in the saucepan, pour in the liquid and bring to a boil over high heat. Cover the saucepan tightly and reduce the heat to maintain a gentle simmer. Quinoa generally needs to be cooked for about 15 minutes and is finished when it's just tender and you can see a little curlicue in each piece.

RESTING AND FLUFFING: After cooking, let the quinoa rest off the heat in the lidded saucepan for 10 minutes. For the very best results, drape a clean kitchen towel just over the surface of the quinoa and replace the lid on the top. The towel will absorb any excess moisture and save the quinoa from the slightest hint of sogginess.

After 10 minutes, remove the lid and towel and use a fork to fluff the quinoa, gently separating the pieces. The quinoa is now ready to eat plain or mix into a recipe.

PREPARING AHEAD: A pot of simply cooked quinoa in the refrigerator is a valuable resource during busy times. It keeps well, tightly covered, for up to a week—though with all the enticing ways to use it, it's unlikely to last that long. Cooked quinoa also freezes beautifully (see the box on the facing page).

NOTES ON OTHER INGREDIENTS

EGGS: The recipes throughout this book use large, free-range eggs. Large eggs typically weigh 2 oz. (57g), the equivalent of 3¼ tablespoons. Free-range eggs means that the hens that laid them are uncaged and have some access to outdoor space, hopefully allowing them to engage in natural behaviors.

BUTTER: When you recreate these recipes, the butter used should be unsalted unless otherwise stated in the recipe. This allows you to control the salt level in your cooking and customize it to your taste by adding as much or as little salt as you like. Salted butter can also mask other flavors, therefore downplaying the taste of the rest of your ingredients.

SALT: All recipes in the book use table salt unless noted. The grains of table salt are finer and more uniform than other types of salt, and this allows them to be more evenly distributed.

SUGAR: Unless otherwise specified, granulated white sugar is the sugar used in all recipes. Granulated sugar gives the best baking results, as the larger crystals allow more air into the mixture, therefore creating a lighter texture.

FRUITS AND VEGETABLES: For fruits and vegetables that vary in size (e.g. potatoes, onions, carrots), please assume that they are medium-sized unless otherwise stated in the recipe.

WHEN A RECIPE CALLS FOR UNCOOKED QUINOA, ALWAYS RINSE IT BEFORE USE.

BREAKFAST & BRUNCH

CACAO QUINOA PROTEIN SHAKE

TOASTED COCONUT AND QUINOA BREAKFAST PUDDING

PECAN QUINOA PORRIDGE

VANILLA CARDAMOM QUINOA GRANOLA

QUINOA PANCAKES WITH SPICED STRAWBERRY COMPOTE AND YOGURT

QUINOA CRÊPES WITH BERRIES AND RICOTTA

QUINOA WAFFLES WITH BERRY COMPOTE

QUINOA, FETA CHEESE, AND SPINACH BREAKFAST MUFFINS

QUINOA, CHEDDAR, AND CHIVE MINI FRITTATAS

QUINOA CHICKPEA SCRAMBLE BURRITO

Recipe on page 38

CACAO QUINOA PROTEIN SHAKE

MAKES	2
PREP	5 minutes

YOU WILL NEED

2 large frozen bananas, broken into pieces

3 tablespoons cacao nibs, plus extra for garnish

3 tablespoons cacao powder

3 Medjool dates, pitted and chopped

2 tablespoons quinoa flour

1 tablespoon almond butter

1 teaspoon maca powder

1 cup (240 ml) nondairy milk

1 teaspoon agave nectar (optional)

ice (optional)

FREE FROM
DAIRY, GLUTEN & WHEAT

WHEN YOU WORK HARD, YOU NEED TO REPLENISH YOURSELF IN THE RIGHT WAY. QUINOA FLOUR AND ALMOND BUTTER ARE USED TO GIVE A PROTEIN BOOST TO A RICH, CHOCOLATY, NATURALLY SWEETENED SMOOTHIE.

1 Put all of the ingredients into a high-speed blender and purée until very smooth. Pour into two glasses and sprinkle a few cacao nibs on top of each smoothie. Serve immediately.

TOASTED COCONUT AND QUINOA BREAKFAST PUDDING

SERVES	4
PREP	10 minutes
COOK	35 minutes

YOU WILL NEED

1 can (14 oz./400 g) coconut milk

1¾ cups (420 ml) coconut milk drink

¼ cup (60 ml) maple syrup

¾ cup (150 g) uncooked quinoa

1 teaspoon ground cinnamon

½ cup (37 g) toasted coconut

FREE FROM
DAIRY, GLUTEN & WHEAT

THIS IS CREAMY COMFORT FOOD YOU WILL WANT TO WAKE UP FOR. MILDLY SWEET, LIKE A TOASTED MARSHMALLOW, THIS PROTEIN-PACKED BREAKFAST WILL KEEP YOU GOING ALL DAY.

1 Bring the coconut milks and maple syrup to a boil in a large saucepan, whisking often and watching carefully so the mixture does not boil over. Add the quinoa and bring the mixture to a boil, again taking care it does not boil over. Once it boils, reduce to the lowest heat and cover. Continue to watch the mixture for signs of over boiling for the first few minutes. Stir occasionally.

2 Cook, covered, for 25 minutes. After 25 minutes, uncover and increase the heat slightly, stir in the cinnamon and toasted coconut, and continue to cook for another 5 minutes, uncovered. Serve immediately.

THE BEST OF BOTH WORLDS: This recipe uses coconut milk from carton and can—the carton milk cuts down on calories, while the canned milk adds richness.

QUINOA BREAKFAST PUDDING VARIATIONS

IT'S EASY TO CUSTOMIZE YOUR BREAKFAST PUDDING BY USING CLASSIC FLAVOR COMBINATIONS. TRY THESE ALTERNATIVE FLAVOR VARIATIONS THAT TASTE SO GOOD THEY COULD EASILY DOUBLE AS DESSERT!

MAPLE SESAME GINGER BREAKFAST PUDDING

For a sweet-and-savory version of this breakfast, stir in 1 tablespoon tahini and ½ inch (1.2 cm) fresh ginger root, peeled and minced fine, after the quinoa mixture has cooked for 25 minutes. Omit the cinnamon and coconut and continue cooking as in the main recipe on page 24.

BLUEBERRY LEMON BREAKFAST PUDDING

For a refreshing twist, try swapping out the cinnamon and coconut for some fresh fruits. Stir in ½ cup (75 g) fresh blueberries and the juice of 1 lemon after the quinoa mixture has cooked for 25 minutes, and continue cooking as in the main recipe on page 24. Serve with a few more fresh berries on top.

WARM CARDAMOM ROSE PUDDING

For a fragrant breakfast that could double as dessert, stir in 2 drops rosewater, 2 teaspoons cardamom, and 1 teaspoon saffron in place of the cinnamon and coconut, and continue cooking as in the main recipe on page 24. This pudding would also be a great end to a Moroccan or Lebanese meal.

TAHINI

Tahini is a nutrient-dense superfood with a long list of benefits. In addition to being a great source of calcium, good fats, and many minerals, tahini is a complete protein, packing in more than most nuts. Make use of tahini's versatility in sweet and savory dishes: Whisk with lemon juice and maple syrup for an easy salad dressing, spread on warm toast, or stir into your morning oatmeal.

PECAN QUINOA PORRIDGE

SERVES	4
PREP	5 minutes
COOK	30 minutes

YOU WILL NEED

1 pint (450 ml) skim milk, plus extra for serving

¼ teaspoon sea salt

scant 1 cup (180 g) uncooked quinoa

2 tablespoons maple syrup, plus extra for serving

½ teaspoon ground cinnamon

scant ⅔ cup (75 g) chopped pecan nuts

FREE FROM
GLUTEN & WHEAT

THIS IS A FABULOUS GLUTEN-FREE PORRIDGE WITH MAPLE SYRUP AND PECANS. THE QUINOA AND SKIM MILK MAKE IT A HEARTY YET HEALTHY BREAKFAST OPTION.

1 Bring the milk to a boil in a large saucepan, then reduce the heat and add the salt. Add the quinoa, mix well, and bring back to a boil before covering and simmering gently for 15–20 minutes.

2 Remove the lid, add the maple syrup and cinnamon, and continue to cook over low heat for another 10 minutes, or until the quinoa porridge is thick and creamy with very little liquid left.

3 Remove from the heat, add the pecans, and serve immediately with extra maple syrup and milk.

QUINOA PORRIDGE VARIATIONS

ADD SOME MORE IDEAS TO THE QUINOA PORRIDGE POT WITH THESE VARIATIONS. QUINOA PORRIDGE MAKES THE PERFECT HEALTHY SNACK OUTSIDE OF BREAKFAST TIME, TOO.

DAIRY-FREE QUINOA PORRIDGE WITH HONEY AND TOASTED ALMONDS

Use almond milk in place of cow's milk, and replace the maple syrup with 2 tablespoons organic honey. Lightly toast I cup (70 g) sliced almonds in a nonstick skillet until just golden brown, and sprinkle over the porridge for serving. Serve with extra almond milk and honey. Soy or oat milk can also be used in place of the almond milk.

SUMMER FRUIT AND BERRY QUINOA PORRIDGE WITH BROWN SUGAR AND VANILLA

Make the porridge as in the main recipe on page 28, but omit the cinnamon and add 2 teaspoons vanilla extract instead. Omit the maple syrup too, and add 2 tablespoons light brown sugar, such as demerara. Cook the porridge for another I0 minutes after adding the vanilla and brown sugar, stirring constantly so the sugar dissolves. Serve immediately with I⅔ cups (250 g) of mixed summer fruit and berries such as halved strawberries, raspberries, blueberries, cherries, and chopped peaches divided between the four bowls. Offer a bowl of brown sugar for people to add themselves.

OAT AND QUINOA PORRIDGE WITH PECANS AND DRIED APRICOTS

Cook ½ cup (100 g) quinoa and ¾ cup (75 g) oats together as in the main recipe, with I pint (450 ml) oat milk in place of skim milk. When the porridge is thick and creamy, add ½ cup (80 g) chopped dried apricots along with the maple syrup, cinnamon, and pecans, and mix well. Serve immediately with extra oat milk.

NUTS

Nuts not only taste delicious, but they are also an essential ingredient in lots of baking recipes, as well as being fabulous when added to salads and savory dishes. High in dietary fiber and minerals such as potassium and magnesium, they are also rich in bone-building calcium and protein. Scatter them over desserts, pancakes, porridge, and salads for an extra-healthy boost, or add them to sweet bakes, tarts, and cakes for an afternoon tea treat. They are also delicious when roasted in honey and served as a snack with cocktails.

VANILLA CARDAMOM QUINOA GRANOLA

MAKES	5 cups
PREP	10 minutes
COOK	40 minutes, plus cooling

YOU WILL NEED

2 cups (200 g) gluten-free rolled oats

1 cup (200 g) uncooked quinoa

1 cup (120 g) shelled unsalted pistachios

¼ cup (60 ml) canola oil

½ cup (120 ml) mild honey

2 tablespoons vanilla extract

1½ teaspoons ground cinnamon

¾ teaspoon ground cardamom

¼ teaspoon fine sea salt

1 cup sliced almonds

FREE FROM
DAIRY, GLUTEN
& WHEAT

THIS GRANOLA IS SATISFYING AND LIGHTLY SWEET. THE OATS, QUINOA, AND WHOLE AND SLICED NUTS GIVE IT A GREAT TEXTURE WITH A FEW DIFFERENT TYPES OF CRUNCH. TO MAKE IT GLUTEN-FREE, BE SURE TO USE CERTIFIED GLUTEN-FREE OATS.

1 Preheat the oven to 325°F/170°C/Gas Mark 3. Line a cookie sheet with parchment.

2 In a large mixing bowl, toss together the oats, quinoa, and pistachios. Pour in the canola oil and honey and mix well to coat evenly.

3 Sprinkle the vanilla, cinnamon, cardamom, and salt over the mixture, then stir well to distribute.

4 Pour the granola onto the cookie sheet and spread in an even layer. Bake for 20 minutes. Briefly remove from the oven and gently, but thoroughly, stir in the sliced almonds, then spread again in an even layer. Return to the oven and continue baking until golden brown, about 20 minutes more. The granola should be gently crisp, but will crisp up more while cooling. Let cool on the sheet, then break apart and store in an airtight container at room temperature for up to 3 weeks.

SLIPPERY SLOPE: Measure the oil first, then measure the honey in the same measuring cup. The honey will slide right out.

QUINOA GRANOLA VARIATIONS
WITH A FEW TWEAKS, THIS GRANOLA RECIPE CAN TAKE ON A VARIETY OF DIFFERENT FLAVORS AND PERSONALITIES. HERE ARE SOME FAVORITES.

STRAWBERRY APRICOT
Immediately after baking, toss in ¾ cup (105 g) diced dried strawberries and ¾ cup (120 g) chopped dried apricots. The flavors will meld while the granola cools.

DARK CHOCOLATE CHERRY
Immediately after baking, toss in ¾ cup (95 g) dried cherries in with the granola mix. Once theit has cooled, toss in ¾ cup (115 g) mini dark chocolate chips or 4 oz. (115 g) chopped dark chocolate.

SPICED APPLE
Replace the pistachios and almonds with 2 cups (240 g) chopped walnuts or pecans. Replace the cardamom with ¼ teaspoon ground nutmeg, ¼ teaspoon ground allspice, and ¼ teaspoon ground cloves. Immediately after baking, stir in ¾ cup (100 g) chopped dried apples.

CARDAMOM

Cardamom can be an under-appreciated spice. At once warming and bracing, it's an easy way to impart a special fragrance to sweet and savory foods alike. This recipe uses pre-ground cardamom, which is much less strong than if you grind your own. If you choose to grind your own cardamom, start with green pods rather than black. Peel off the pods and grind only the seeds in a mortar and pestle. You'll only need seeds from about 3 pods to equal the flavor of ¾ teaspoon of preground spice.

QUINOA PANCAKES WITH SPICED STRAWBERRY COMPOTE AND YOGURT

SERVES	4
PREP	10 minutes
COOK	30 minutes

YOU WILL NEED

2 eggs

1 cup (240 ml) well-shaken buttermilk

¾ cup (180 ml) whole milk

1 cup (180 g) cooked quinoa

2 cups (240 g) whole-wheat pastry flour

¼ teaspoon fine sea salt

1 teaspoon baking powder

½ teaspoon baking soda

3 tablespoons maple syrup

2 tablespoons butter, melted

nonstick cooking spray, for greasing

⅔ cup (175 g) plain Greek-style yogurt, for serving

FOR THE COMPOTE

20 oz. (560 g) hulled fresh strawberries or whole frozen strawberries

¼ cup (60 ml) maple syrup

1 teaspoon minced fresh ginger root

½ teaspoon ground cinnamon

⅛ teaspoon ground cardamom

2 teaspoons vanilla extract

FLUFFY WHOLE-GRAIN BUTTERMILK PANCAKES HARDLY NEED IMPROVEMENT, BUT THE ADDITION OF QUINOA AND A LIGHTLY SPICED COMPOTE MAKES THEM EXTRA SPECIAL.

1 First make the compote. Put the strawberries, maple syrup, ginger, cinnamon, and cardamom into a small saucepan over medium-high heat. Bring to a boil, stirring frequently. Reduce the heat to maintain a brisk simmer, and add the vanilla. Cook until the strawberries are very soft and their liquid has thickened somewhat, around 10 minutes. (The liquid will continue to thicken as it cools.) Remove from the heat and smash some of the strawberries with the back of a spoon. Set to one side to cool slightly.

2 In a medium bowl, beat the eggs with a fork. Beat in the buttermilk and milk. Add the quinoa, flour, salt, baking powder, baking soda, maple syrup, and melted butter. Stir the mixture gently with a fork until there are no noticeable pockets of flour left. The batter will still be slightly lumpy.

3 Coat a nonstick skillet with a thin layer of the nonstick cooking spray and heat over medium-high heat for a few minutes. Drop batter by the ¼-cupful (60 ml) onto the heated skillet, without crowding. The batter should sizzle slightly at first. Cook until the underside is nicely browned and the top has lots of bubbles, 2–3 minutes. Then flip and cook until the other side is browned, 1–2 minutes more. Adjust the heat to cook through without burning, and add additional oil to the skillet as necessary.

4 Serve immediately, topped with spiced strawberry compote and a dollop of yogurt.

DAIRY-FREE BRUNCH
For a dairy-free
version, use your
favorite nondairy milk
and substitute a
neutral tasting oil for
the butter.
   To make nondairy
"buttermilk," combine
1 cup (240 ml) of
nondairy milk with
1 tablespoon fresh
lemon juice or apple
cider vinegar. Stir and
let sit for 10 minutes
before using.

QUINOA CRÊPES WITH BERRIES AND RICOTTA

SERVES	4
PREP	15 minutes, plus resting
COOK	40–50 minutes

YOU WILL NEED

1 cup (125 g) quinoa flour

1 cup (240 ml) unsweetened rice milk

1 egg, beaten

2 cups (300 g) mixed berries (fresh or frozen)

2 tablespoons honey

2 tablespoons water

1 cup (150 g) ricotta

2 tablespoons confectioners' sugar

coconut oil, for frying

strips of lemon zest, for garnish

pinch of salt

(pictured on page 21)

FREE FROM
GLUTEN & WHEAT

MAKING GLUTEN-FREE CRÊPES FOR BREAKFAST (AND DESSERT) IS EASY WITH QUINOA FLOUR. TOPPED WITH SWEET BERRIES AND SOFT CHEESE, THEY'RE AN INDULGENT TREAT.

1 Sift the quinoa flour and salt into a bowl. Whisk the rice milk and egg together, then slowly whisk this into the quinoa flour until you have a smooth, lump-free batter. Cover with a cloth or plastic wrap and let rest for 30 minutes (or overnight in the refrigerator).

2 Add the berries to a saucepan with the honey and water. Gently heat for 5 minutes, stirring every so often, until the berries have just started to break down and are warmed through. Cover and put to one side.

3 Beat the ricotta in a bowl with the confectioners' sugar. Put to one side. Heat the oven to its lowest setting.

4 Warm I tablespoon of coconut oil in a large skillet. Swirl the oil around the skillet to coat the bottom, and pour out any excess. Add a small ladleful of the batter to the skillet. Turn and swirl the skillet so you have a thin pancake that coats the bottom. Fry over medium-high heat for I–2 minutes, until the crêpe is set and golden brown underneath.

5 Loosen the edge of the crêpe with a paring knife or small offset spatula, then flip it over. Fry for another I–2 minutes, until the crêpe has colored underneath. Slide onto an ovenproof plate and keep warm in the oven.

6 Repeat with the rest of the batter, adding more coconut oil as you need it. You should be able to make 8–12 crêpes, depending on how large you make them.

7 Serve the warm quinoa crêpes folded or rolled around the honeyed berries and whipped ricotta, garnished with lemon zest.

QUINOA CRÊPE VARIATIONS

THERE IS MORE THAN ONE WAY TO FILL A CRÊPE. HERE ARE THE FLAVORS FROM TWO CLASSIC DESSERTS TURNED INTO ROLLED-UP TREATS—PLUS A WAY TO MAKE THESE CRÊPES VEGAN.

CHOCOLATE AND CACAO NIB QUINOA CRÊPES

Make the crêpes as in the main recipe, using almond milk instead of rice milk in the batter and adding I teaspoon pumpkin spice or a pinch of cinnamon, ground ginger, and nutmeg to the flour. Fry long slices of banana in coconut oil for I–2 minutes on each side so they just caramelize. Keep them warm in the oven, then fry the crêpes. Serve the crêpes and bananas with some crunchy cacao nibs and spoonfuls of yogurt.

APPLE PIE CRÊPES

Make the crêpes as in the main recipe, using almond milk instead of rice milk in the batter. Make the filling by cooking 6 peeled, cored, and chopped eating apples with ½ teaspoon ground cinnamon, ¼ teaspoon nutmeg, a pinch of ground cloves, 2 tablespoons maple syrup, and I tablespoon water over low heat for 5 minutes, until the apples are a little soft but not pulpy. Toast ½ cup (60 g) walnut pieces in a dry skillet for 2–3 minutes until browned. Serve the apple compote with the crêpes, walnuts, yogurt, and extra maple syrup.

VEGAN QUINOA CRÊPES

Swap the egg for 2 tablespoons melted coconut oil and make the crêpes as per the main recipe. You can use rice, coconut, or soy milk in the batter. Serve the crêpes with mixed berries and coconut or soy yogurt.

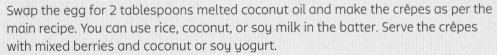

QUINOA WAFFLES WITH BERRY COMPOTE

SERVES	4
PREP	10 minutes
COOK	30 minutes

YOU WILL NEED

nonstick cooking spray,
   for greasing

1 cup (120 g) gluten-free
   flour

½ cup (50 g) gluten-free
   rolled oats

½ cup (65 g) quinoa flour

¾ cup (180 ml) orange juice

¾ cup (180 ml) nondairy
   milk

3 tablespoons olive oil

1½ tablespoons sugar

2 teaspoons baking powder

1 teaspoon vanilla extract

1 teaspoon orange zest

pinch of salt

FOR THE BERRY COMPOTE

1 cup (170 g) diced fresh
   strawberries

1 cup (140 g) fresh
   blackberries

2 tablespoons water

2 tablespoons sugar

1 tablespoon lemon juice

pinch of salt

fresh berries, for serving

FREE FROM
DAIRY, GLUTEN
& WHEAT

FINDING A GOOD GLUTEN-FREE WAFFLE RECIPE IS CHALLENGING, BUT THIS ONE HAS ADDED PROTEIN FROM QUINOA FLOUR AND STILL RETAINS A SLIGHTLY CRUNCHY OUTSIDE WITH A FLUFFY, MOIST INTERIOR.

1 Heat a shallow waffle iron (not Belgian), and make sure that it is hot by adding a couple of drops of water; they must sizzle as they hit the irons. Add a heavy coat of nonstick cooking spray to the irons.

2 Place all of the waffle ingredients in a blender and purée until smooth; set aside for 10 minutes to let the batter thicken.

3 Pour the waffle batter over the iron until mostly covered, close the lid, and cook for 8–10 minutes, following the manufacturer's instructions. Once the iron stops steaming, carefully lift the lid and pull out the waffle. It should be golden brown. Repeat until all of the batter has been used up.

4 While the waffles are cooking, place all of the berry compote ingredients in a small saucepan and bring to a boil over medium heat. Reduce the heat to medium low and simmer for 15 minutes, or until the liquid has turned into a syrup.

5 Divide the waffles between four plates and top with the berry compote. Serve hot.

MAKE AHEAD
You can store these waffles, with parchment between them, in the freezer for 6 months. Reheat them in the toaster just as you would store-bought waffles.

QUINOA WAFFLE VARIATIONS

AN EASY WAY TO CHANGE UP YOUR FAVORITE RECIPES IS TO USE ONLY SEASONAL PRODUCE. STONE FRUITS ARE ALSO AN OPTION IN WARMER MONTHS, WHILE RICHER FLAVORS ARE BETTER SUITED FOR WHEN FRUITS ARE NOT IN ABUNDANCE.

(VG) (DF) (GF) (WF)

PEACHES AND NECTARINES

Whenever they are in season, chop up some fresh peaches and nectarines, in equal parts, and use in the place of the berries in the compote.

(V) (GF) (WF)

CHOCOLATE

These waffles would also be great with a chocolaty switch-up. Follow the main recipe on page 40 but replace ¼ cup (25 g) rolled oats with the same amount of cocoa powder and top with chocolate syrup instead of compote for a decadent brunch recipe.

(V) (GF) (WF)

MAPLE CREAM

Maybe you'd like a richer topping than compote? Try whipping I cup (240 g) cream cheese or cashew cream with 3 tablespoons of maple syrup and a pinch of ground cinnamon for a slightly sweet maple cream.

BERRIES

Berries are high in phytonutrients that keep your heart healthy and have anticancer properties. In one recent study, blackberries were shown to have the highest antioxidant value of any food tested, meaning that they are a powerful free-radical fighter and may have a positive impact on health and lower the risk of certain diseases. Strawberries also pack a surprising nutritional punch. They contain more vitamin C than oranges—roughly 160 percent of your recommended daily allowance in just 1 cup.

QUINOA, FETA CHEESE, AND SPINACH BREAKFAST MUFFINS

MAKES	12
PREP	5 minutes
COOK	20 minutes

YOU WILL NEED

nonstick cooking spray, for greasing

½ cup (100 g) uncooked quinoa

1 cup (240 ml) water

generous 3 cups (375 g) self-rising flour

7 oz. (200 g) spinach leaves, washed, trimmed, and shredded

1⅓ cups (200 g) crumbled feta cheese

1 tablespoon chopped fresh dill

1¼ cups (300 ml) skim milk

8 tablespoons (100 g) butter, melted

1 egg, beaten

salt and black pepper

THESE DELICIOUS AND HEALTHY LITTLE BREAKFAST MUFFINS ARE THE PERFECT WAY TO START THE DAY—AND THEY WILL KEEP YOU GOING UNTIL LUNCHTIME.

1 Preheat the oven to 400°F/200°C/Gas Mark 6. Coat a standard 12-cup muffin pan with the nonstick cooking spray.

2 Put the quinoa in a saucepan with the water. Cover. Bring to a boil, then reduce the heat and gently simmer for 10–15 minutes, or until all the water has been absorbed and the quinoa is tender. If it looks like it's getting too dry while it cooks, add a splash more water. Drain well, and transfer to a bowl to cool.

3 Pour the flour into a large bowl and add the spinach, crumbled feta cheese, cooked quinoa, and dill. Season with salt and black pepper to taste. Stir well to combine.

4 Whisk the milk with the melted butter and beaten egg and pour into the dry ingredients. Mix with a large spoon until just combined—do not overmix as this will result in a tough texture.

5 Spoon the muffin mixture into the muffin pan and bake for 20 minutes, until the muffins are well risen and golden brown.

6 Carefully turn the muffins out onto a wire rack to cool; they are best served warm.

ZIP THEM UP: If you bake more muffins than you need, these muffins can be frozen in a zip-top bag for up to 3 months.

BREAKFAST MUFFIN VARIATIONS

TRY ONE OF THESE THREE EXTRA IDEAS ON HOW TO COOK AND SERVE THESE TASTY MUFFINS—FROM A MEAT LOVER'S VERSION TO THE PERFECT OFFICE-READY PACKED LUNCH, THERE IS SOMETHING FOR EVERYONE.

HAM AND CHEDDAR MUFFINS

Follow the main recipe on page 44. In place of the spinach and feta cheese, add 1 cup (100 g) chopped cooked ham and 2 cups (200 g) shredded cheddar cheese. If you would like a vegetable element, add a scant ½ cup (50 g) sun-dried tomatoes in olive oil, drained and finely chopped. Serve with a crunchy side salad or coleslaw.

HERBY CREAM CHEESE AND SCALLION MUFFIN SANDWICHES

To make the sandwich spread, mix ½ cup (120 g) herb and garlic cream cheese with a small bunch of trimmed and chopped scallions. Season to taste with salt and black pepper, then simply cut the muffins in half and spread with the cream cheese sandwich spread. Serve with salad.

TOMATO, EGG, AND BACON MUFFINS

Breakfast in a muffin! Simply fry (or broil) half a tomato per person in a little olive oil until charred and soft, then place the tomato halves on the bottom half of a cut muffin; fry (or broil) 2 strips of smoked streaky bacon per person and then fry 1 egg per person, in a little olive oil or the bacon fat. Arrange the fried egg and bacon strips on top of the tomato, and place the other half of the cut muffin on top to make a sandwich. Serve with assorted sauces and relishes.

EGGS

Eggs are essential in any cook's kitchen and are a complete protein ingredient; they boast a host of vitamins such as B1, B2, B3, B5, B6, B12, and choline. Rich in folic acid too, they are nature's perfect packet of goodness. Scramble them, poach them, fry them, or coddle them—they are one of the handiest ingredients for an easy, protein-rich breakfast, as well as being a requirement in most cake recipes due to their emulsifying properties.

QUINOA, CHEDDAR, AND CHIVE MINI FRITTATAS

MAKES	12
PREP	10 minutes
COOK	25 minutes

YOU WILL NEED

nonstick cooking spray or butter, for greasing

1½ cups cooked quinoa

6 tablespoons minced fresh chives

12 eggs

½ teaspoon fine sea salt

4 oz. (115 g) extra-sharp cheddar, shredded

black pepper

FREE FROM
GLUTEN & WHEAT

MAKING FRITTATAS IN A MUFFIN PAN SETS YOU UP WITH A WEEK'S WORTH OF PORTABLE AND NUTRITIOUS BREAKFASTS AND LUNCHES. QUINOA ADDS HEFT AND FIBER, SO YOU'LL STAY SATISFIED WHILE USING FEWER EGGS.

1 Preheat the oven to 350°F/180°C/Gas Mark 4 with a rack in the center. Generously spray or butter a standard 12-cup muffin pan.

2 Place 2 tablespoons of quinoa into each muffin cup. Divide the chives equally among the cups.

3 Crack the eggs into a medium bowl, add the salt and a few good grinds of black pepper, and beat with a fork until well combined. Divide the eggs equally among the muffin cups.

4 Divide the cheese among the muffin cups. Use a teaspoon to pop any bubbles and to gently distribute the cheese and chives into each frittata mix.

5 Bake for about 20–25 minutes, until the eggs are just set all the way through. (Test with a knife or cake tester.)

6 Let rest for 5 minutes, then gently loosen the frittatas with a silicone spatula. Serve warm from the oven or remove to a wire rack to cool completely.

FOR LUNCH: Try serving these frittatas with a side salad for a light lunch.

MINI FRITTATA VARIATIONS

SINCE QUINOA AND EGGS BOTH PAIR WELL WITH MANY FLAVORS, THE SKY'S THE LIMIT ON INTRODUCING NEW INGREDIENTS INTO THESE FRITTATAS. JUST KEEP THE TOTAL VOLUME CONSISTENT SO THEY FIT IN THE MUFFIN CUPS.

(V) (GF) (WF)

ROASTED RED BELL PEPPER AND FRESH GOAT CHEESE

Mince I roasted red bell pepper and add to the muffin cups on top of the quinoa per the main recipe on page 48. Replace the cheddar with crumbled fresh goat cheese.

(V) (GF) (WF)

SHALLOT AND GRUYÈRE

Sauté 2 shallots in I tablespoon olive oil, and add to the frittatas in place of the chives per the main recipe. Swap in shredded Gruyère for the cheddar.

(V) (GF) (WF)

SUN-DRIED TOMATO AND MOZZARELLA

Soak 3 sun-dried tomatoes in hot water for IO minutes to soften. Mince and sprinkle over the quinoa per the main recipe. Replace the chives with strips of fresh basil. Replace the cheddar with diced fresh mozzarella and ¼ cup (25 g) vegetarian Parmesan cheese, added to the eggs before beating.

QUINOA CHICKPEA SCRAMBLE BURRITO

SERVES	4
PREP	10 minutes
COOK	30 minutes

YOU WILL NEED

1¾ cups (420 ml) vegetable stock

¾ cup (150 g) uncooked red quinoa

2 tablespoons coconut oil

8 oz. (225 g) russet potatoes, diced

1 cup (160 g) diced onion

1 can (14 oz./400 g) chickpeas, drained and rinsed

3 tablespoons nutritional yeast

¼ teaspoon black salt/Kala Namak (optional)

1 cup (180 g) fresh diced tomatoes

3 cups (90 g) baby spinach

4 large whole-wheat tortillas

salt and black pepper

lime wedges and salsa, for serving

(pictured on page 52)

CHICKPEAS AND QUINOA ARE SUPER NUTRITIOUS AND TASTY WHEN COMBINED WITH POTATOES AND SPINACH. WRAPPING THEM UP INTO A BURRITO CREATES A GREAT ON-THE-GO MEAL.

1 Put the vegetable stock and red quinoa in a large saucepan, cover with a lid, and bring to a boil over medium heat. Reduce to medium-low heat and simmer for 20–25 minutes, or until all the liquid is gone and the quinoa is tender.

2 While the quinoa is cooking, warm the coconut oil in a large skillet over medium heat. Once hot, add the potatoes to the skillet and cook for 15 minutes, stirring occasionally so that the potatoes don't stick to the skillet or burn.

3 Reduce the heat to medium low and add the onion, sautéing for 10 more minutes, or until the potatoes are cooked through.

4 Next, mash the chickpeas in a bowl with the nutritional yeast and black salt, if using, and then add to the potatoes. Cook for 5 minutes, then stir in the tomatoes and spinach, and continue heating until the spinach becomes slightly wilted.

5 Season the mixture with salt and black pepper. Carefully fold the cooked quinoa into the potato mixture, then evenly distribute the filling between the four tortillas. Fold one side and what will be the bottom of the tortilla in toward each other, and then roll tightly to make the burrito. Serve with lime wedges and your favorite salsa.

FREE FROM DAIRY

EASY DOES IT
Warm the tortillas in the oven or microwave slightly before folding them, so they are more pliable and less likely to tear.

QUINOA SCRAMBLE VARIATIONS

WHILE NEARLY EVERYONE CAN GET ON BOARD WITH BREAKFAST BURRITOS, IT'S ALWAYS A GOOD IDEA TO HAVE SOME ALTERNATIVES ON HAND AND OFFER SOME VARIETY FOR THOSE WHO ARE A LITTLE HARDER TO PLEASE.

TOFU QUINOA SCRAMBLE

If you don't like chickpeas try replacing them with 12 oz. (350 g) extra-firm tofu (cut into cubes), which is a lean protein, or 3 scrambled eggs for a vegetarian version. Omit the nutritional yeast and black salt.

GLUTEN-FREE BREAKFAST BOWL

For a gluten-free version, make this recipe into a deliciously satisfying breakfast bowl by eliminating the tortillas, or using large collard leaves in place of the tortillas.

MEXICAN BEAN AND CHILI BURRITOS

Give these burritos some Mexican flair by using the same amount of salsa instead of tomatoes, black beans instead of chickpeas, and adding some chili powder and cumin to the filling.

SNACKS & APPETIZERS

QUINOA-DUSTED TORTILLA CHIPS WITH ARTICHOKE ARUGULA DIP

SMOKY EGGPLANT AND QUINOA DIP

PUMPED-UP FIVE-LAYER QUINOA DIP

CHEESY BUFFALO QUINOA TOTS

PUFFED QUINOA BHELPURI

SWEET POTATO QUINOA KIBBEH

SOUTHWESTERN QUINOA LETTUCE CUPS

QUINOA-COATED FISH STICK SANDWICH

VEGGIE AND QUINOA SUMMER ROLLS
WITH CAJUN TAHINI SAUCE

QUINOA CRAB CAKES

Recipe on page 66

QUINOA-DUSTED TORTILLA CHIPS WITH ARTICHOKE ARUGULA DIP

SERVES	4
PREP	20 minutes
COOK	30 minutes

YOU WILL NEED

3 tablespoons quinoa flour

1 teaspoon onion powder

8 corn tortillas

1 tablespoon olive oil

¼ teaspoon fine salt

FOR THE DIP

1 cup (170 g) cooked white beans, rinsed

½ cup (120 ml) water

2 tablespoons olive oil

3 tablespoons quinoa flour

1½ tablespoons nutritional yeast, plus extra for topping

2 teaspoons lemon juice

½ teaspoon sea salt

pinch of freshly ground black pepper

1 can (14 oz./400 g) artichoke hearts in brine, drained

2 cups baby arugula, lightly packed

chopped fresh cilantro, for garnish

FREE FROM
DAIRY, GLUTEN & WHEAT

QUINOA FLOUR ADDS A SUBTLE NUTTY FLAVOR TO BAKED CORN TORTILLA CHIPS AND HELPS TO THICKEN THE DIP, TOO. SERVE BOTH OF THESE WARM AND YOU HAVE AN IMMEDIATE CROWD-PLEASER AT ANY GET-TOGETHER.

1 Preheat the oven to 375°F/190°C/Gas Mark 5 and have ready a large cookie sheet or two smaller cookie sheets.

2 Stir the quinoa flour and onion powder together in a shallow bowl. Brush each tortilla with a light coating of olive oil on each side, then lay it on top of the quinoa flour and press down gently, applying a thin coating of flour on each side.

3 When all the tortillas are lightly coated with quinoa flour, lay them out on the cookie sheet(s) in a single layer and sprinkle with salt (you'll probably need to work in batches). Bake for 10–12 minutes, or until the tortillas are golden; some will have bubbled slightly. Set on a rack to cool. Leave the oven on, as you will need it to bake the dip.

4 Place all of the dip ingredients, except for the artichokes and arugula, in a food processor and purée until completely smooth. Add the artichokes to the food processor and pulse until the pieces are small, then transfer to a small ovenproof casserole dish. Fold in the arugula, top with ½ teaspoon of nutritional yeast and bake for 15 minutes. Wait 5 minutes for the dip to cool slightly before garnishing with cilantro and serving with the chips.

SMOKY EGGPLANT AND QUINOA DIP

SERVES	4
PREP	10 minutes
COOK	1 hour

YOU WILL NEED

1¼ cups (250 g) uncooked red quinoa

2 large eggplants

4 tablespoons extra-virgin olive oil

4 garlic cloves, peeled

scant ½ cup (80 g) black olives, pitted and roughly chopped

¾ cup (80 g) sun-dried tomatoes in oil, drained and roughly chopped

2 tablespoons fresh marjoram, finely chopped

zest and juice of 1 lemon

1 tablespoon balsamic vinegar

salt and black pepper

fresh crusty bread, or vegetable crudités, for serving

FREE FROM
DAIRY, GLUTEN & WHEAT

THIS SMOKY DIP MADE WITH RED QUINOA, EGGPLANT, SUN-DRIED TOMATOES, AND PLUMP OLIVES MAKES A WONDERFUL VEGETARIAN SANDWICH FILLING AS WELL AS THE PERFECT SAUCE FOR PASTA OR ROASTED VEGETABLES.

1 Preheat the oven to 425°F/220°C/Gas Mark 7.

2 Put the quinoa in a saucepan with 1¼ cups (300 ml) of cold water. Cover. Bring to a boil, then reduce the heat and gently simmer for 10–15 minutes, or until all the water has been absorbed and the quinoa is tender. If it looks like it's getting too dry while it cooks, add a splash more water. Drain well and transfer to a bowl.

3 Meanwhile, cut the eggplants in half lengthwise and score the flesh on the inside. Put them in a roasting tray and drizzle with 3 tablespoons of olive oil. Bake for 45–50 minutes, until the flesh is soft, adding the garlic cloves for the last 10 minutes. Let cool.

4 Scoop out the flesh of the eggplants and add to a bowl with the garlic, cooked quinoa, and the rest of the ingredients. Mix well.

5 Adjust the seasoning to taste with the salt and pepper, and serve warm or at room temperature with crusty bread, or try fresh crudités for a gluten-free option.

PUMPED-UP FIVE-LAYER QUINOA DIP

SERVES	4
PREP	17 minutes
COOK	20 minutes

YOU WILL NEED

1 cup (200 g) uncooked quinoa

1½ cups (360 ml) tomato juice

1 can (14 oz./400 g) refried beans

⅓ cup (20 g) nutritional yeast

1 fresh jalapeño, seeded and chopped

½ head iceberg lettuce, chopped

2 tomatoes, diced

1 avocado, pitted and cubed

tortilla chips, for serving

FREE FROM
DAIRY, GLUTEN
& WHEAT

THIS BRIGHTLY COLORED CROWD-PLEASING PARTY FAVORITE IS A PROTEIN-PACKED UPDATE ON AN OLD CLASSIC AND WILL BE WELCOME AT ANY GATHERING!

1 In a medium pot over high heat, bring the quinoa and tomato juice to a rolling boil. Reduce the heat to a simmer, cover, and cook for 20 minutes. Remove from the heat and fluff with a fork.

2 In a medium bowl, combine the refried beans with the nutritional yeast and chopped jalapeño.

3 You can make individual servings as shown, or for a bigger gathering, use a large shallow bowl or baking dish (8 × 8 inch/ 20 × 20 cm), and spread the refried bean-jalapeño mixture evenly to create a base layer. Spoon the tomato quinoa over the beans evenly as the second layer. The third layer is the chopped lettuce, followed by the diced tomatoes and avocado cubes. Serve with tortilla chips.

PARTY PERFECT: Use small glasses or plastic cups to make individual servings—great for a stand-up party.

CHEESY BUFFALO QUINOA TOTS

MAKES	20
PREP	15 minutes, plus freezing
COOK	25 minutes

YOU WILL NEED

3 oz. (85 g) nondairy mozzarella

1 can (14 oz./400 g) cannellini beans, drained and rinsed

1½ cups (270 g) cooked quinoa (cooked in vegetable stock)

1 garlic clove, minced

salt and black pepper

½ cup (120 ml) gluten-free hot sauce or buffalo wing sauce

½ teaspoon celery salt

½ teaspoon paprika

FREE FROM
DAIRY, GLUTEN & WHEAT

THESE FLUFFY, SPICY BITES CAN BE SERVED AS FINGER FOOD WITH DRINKS OR AS A FIRST COURSE. EITHER WAY, THEY ARE FLAVORFUL AND DIPPABLE. SERVE WITH A COOL RANCH DIP TO BALANCE THE SPICY BUFFALO WING FLAVOR.

1 Cut the mozzarella into small ½-inch (1.3 cm) cubes and freeze for at least 1 hour or longer if possible, so that they take on a firmer consistency.

2 Preheat the oven to 350°F/180°C/Gas Mark 4. Line a cookie sheet with parchment.

3 In a food processor, process the beans to a crumbly paste, about 30 seconds. Scrape down the sides using a silicone spatula, add ½ cup of cooked quinoa, and then process for another 30 seconds.

4 Transfer the mixture to a mixing bowl, and combine with the remaining 1 cup of quinoa, the garlic, ½ teaspoon each of salt and black pepper, ¼ cup (60 ml) of hot sauce, the celery salt, and paprika.

5 With your hands, scoop out a 1-inch (2.5 cm) piece of dough, and mold it into a rustic ball shape around a frozen cube of cheese. Place on the cookie sheet.

6 Continue to make balls, spacing them 1 inch (2.5 cm) apart on the cookie sheet, until all of the quinoa mixture and cheese are used.

7 Bake the tots for 15 minutes, then brush with the remaining hot sauce and bake for another 10 minutes.

8 Let the tots sit for several minutes to cool before serving; otherwise, the cheese will be very hot and runny, and the tots will fall apart.

QUINOA TOTS VARIATIONS

CHEESY TOTS ARE THE IDEAL WAY TO CRAM YOUR FAVORITE FLAVORS INTO A PROTEIN-PACKED, HAND-HELD PARTY SNACK. TRY PIZZA, JALAPEÑO PEPPER, OR BROCCOLI-CHEDDAR FLAVORS FOR JUST AS MUCH TASTE AND FUN.

CHEESY PIZZA TOTS

To the bean-quinoa mixture in the main recipe on page 62, add ¼ cup (60 ml) tomato paste and 1 small bunch chopped fresh basil in place of the hot sauce, celery salt, and paprika.

JALAPEÑO PEPPER TOTS

To the bean-quinoa mixture in the main recipe, add 2 fresh jalapeño peppers, finely diced, in place of the hot sauce, celery salt, and paprika.

BROCCOLI-CHEDDAR TOTS

To the bean-quinoa mixture in the main recipe, add ¾ cup (135 g) broccoli florets, chopped fine, in place of the hot sauce, celery salt, and paprika. Wrap around frozen cubes of cheddar instead of mozzarella.

BROCCOLI
Broccoli is a superfood powerhouse, rich in many vitamins and minerals, and a flavonoid that makes broccoli an anti-inflammatory wonder as well. Many like broccoli florets best as a raw dippable snack, while others enjoy them lightly steamed. Roasting or blackening brings a great flavor, and combining broccoli with cheese is a winning combination!

PUFFED QUINOA BHELPURI

MAKES	8
PREP	30 minutes
COOK	5 minutes

YOU WILL NEED

1½ cups (50 g) puffed quinoa

1 red onion, peeled and diced

2 tomatoes, cored and diced

4 poppadums, broken up into small pieces

¼ cup (45 g) chopped dried dates

handful of fresh cilantro, stalks and leaves, chopped

handful of fresh mint, leaves chopped

½ cup (100 g) pomegranate seeds

2 teaspoons cumin seeds

juice of 1 lime

1 tablespoon tamarind paste

1 teaspoon demerara sugar

salt

FREE FROM
DAIRY, GLUTEN & WHEAT

BHELPURI IS A SAVORY INDIAN SNACK MADE FROM PUFFED RICE AND SERVED IN PAPER CONES. THIS VERSION USING QUINOA IS JUST AS DELICIOUS AND MAKES A GREAT NIBBLE WITH DRINKS.

1 Warm a dry skillet over medium heat and pour in the puffed quinoa. Stir and cook for 1–2 minutes, until the quinoa turns golden and smells nutty. Transfer to a large bowl.

2 Stir the red onion, tomatoes, poppadums, dates, cilantro, mint, and pomegranate seeds into the quinoa.

3 Put the cumin seeds into the skillet. Stir and cook over medium heat for 1–2 minutes, until the seeds smell nutty and begin popping. Add them to the quinoa mixture.

4 Whisk the lime juice with the tamarind paste, sugar, and a pinch of salt. Taste and add more salt and sugar if you think it needs it. Stir into the bhelpuri and serve immediately.

PUFF IT UP:
Puffed (or popped) quinoa is made by heating grains of quinoa until they pop. They are great as a cereal or for adding crunch to salads and dishes like this bhelpuri.

To make puffed quinoa, heat a saucepan over medium heat and add a handful of the grains so that they coat the base in one layer. Cover the saucepan and heat the quinoa, shaking it every so often as you would for popcorn, until you can hear it beginning to pop. Keep shaking the saucepan and once the popping starts to slow down, take it off the heat and transfer the quinoa to a bowl. Let it cool, then store in an airtight container and use within a couple of days.

For a crisper result, warm 1 tablespoon sunflower or vegetable oil in the saucepan before adding the quinoa.

KEEP IT FRESH
The dressing is a tangy combination of tamarind, lime juice, and a pinch of sugar. Add it just before serving so the poppadums and quinoa stay crunchy.

SWEET POTATO QUINOA KIBBEH

SERVES	4–8
PREP	20 minutes
COOK	1 hour

YOU WILL NEED

3 sweet potatoes, peeled and chopped into small chunks

½ cup (100 g) uncooked quinoa

big handful of fresh cilantro stalks and leaves, chopped

1 teaspoon allspice

1 teaspoon ground cumin

1 teaspoon ground coriander

pinch of cayenne pepper

1 small onion, finely chopped

⅓ cup (40 g) pine nuts, toasted

extra-virgin olive oil

salt and black pepper

salad leaves, for serving

FREE FROM
DAIRY, GLUTEN & WHEAT

IN THE LEVANT, KIBBEH IS A DEEP-FRIED SNACK MADE WITH LAMB. THIS VERSION IS A HEALTHY VEGAN TAKE USING NUTS AND GRAINS, ALL BOUND TOGETHER WITH SWEET POTATO.

1 Preheat the oven to 350°F/180°C/Gas Mark 4.

2 Bring a large saucepan of water to a boil and add the chopped sweet potatoes. Cover and simmer for 10 minutes, until the potatoes are just starting to soften.

3 Add the quinoa to the sweet potatoes. Simmer for another 10–15 minutes, until both are tender and the sweet potatoes are soft when you press them with a fork. Drain well.

4 Put the sweet potatoes and quinoa back into the saucepan. Mash over low heat until the sweet potatoes are smooth and any excess water has evaporated.

5 Add the fresh cilantro, allspice, cumin, coriander, cayenne pepper, onion, and pine nuts to the saucepan with a good pinch of salt and black pepper. Stir the mixture together. Taste and add more seasoning if you think it needs it.

6 Grease a 2-pint (1-liter) ovenproof dish with a splash of olive oil. Spoon the kibbeh into the dish and smooth over the top. Bake for 30 minutes, or until the top is golden brown.

7 Mark the kibbeh into slices as soon as it comes out of the oven— four, six, or eight slices, depending on how many people you want to serve.

8 Leave the kibbeh in its dish for 10–15 minutes to cool a little before serving with salad.

SOUTHWESTERN QUINOA LETTUCE CUPS

MAKES	10
PREP	10 minutes
COOK	30 minutes

YOU WILL NEED

1½ cups (360 ml) vegetable stock

½ cup (100 g) uncooked tricolor quinoa

½ tablespoon chili powder

2 teaspoons ground cumin

½ teaspoon smoked paprika

½ teaspoon ground coriander

½ teaspoon sea salt

⅛ teaspoon cayenne pepper

2 teaspoons avocado oil

½ cup diced red onion

½ cup (75 g) diced yellow or orange bell pepper

1 cup (170 g) cooked black beans or kidney beans, rinsed and drained

½ cup (90 g) roasted corn (thawed if frozen)

¼ cup (15 g) fresh cilantro, chopped

1 tablespoon lime juice

10 butter lettuce leaves

salt and black pepper

lime wedges, for garnish

FREE FROM
DAIRY, GLUTEN & WHEAT

THESE LEAVES ARE GREAT FOR SERVING AT PARTIES BECAUSE OF THEIR SIZE, AND YOU DON'T NEED UTENSILS TO EAT THEM.

1 Put the vegetable stock, quinoa, chili powder, cumin, paprika, coriander, ½ teaspoon of sea salt, and cayenne pepper in a saucepan, cover, and bring to a boil over medium heat. Reduce to medium-low heat and simmer for 20 minutes, or until all of the liquid is gone and the quinoa is tender.

2 In a large skillet, warm the avocado oil over medium heat. Once hot, add the red onion to the skillet and sauté for 3 minutes, or until mostly translucent. Next, add the bell pepper, black beans, and corn. Cook for an additional 2 minutes, stirring occasionally.

3 Adjust the heat to medium low and add the cooked quinoa to the skillet. Season with salt and black pepper, then incorporate the cilantro and lime juice into the mixture.

4 Divide the filling between the lettuce leaves, garnish each lettuce cup with a lime wedge, and serve immediately.

SERVING STYLE: Different kinds of lettuce will provide more cup-like shapes, although softer lettuce is less messy to eat as you can roll it as you go. Serve each leaf in a silicone muffin cup if you prefer.

QUINOA LETTUCE CUP VARIATIONS

HAVING A RECIPE THAT IS MADE UP OF A FILLING AND SHELL MEANS THAT YOU CAN EASILY CHANGE THE VESSEL OR ADD SOME FLAIR TO THE FILLING WITHOUT TOO MUCH COMPROMISE.

ASIAN-INSPIRED

To make an Asian-inspired version of these lettuce cups, substitute 1 teaspoon fresh ginger root for the spices, replace the black beans with edamame or grilled chicken (for a non-vegan version), use water chestnuts instead of corn, and toss the filling in ¼ cup (60 g) hoisin sauce and 1 teaspoon liquid aminos.

TACO SHELLS

This Southwestern quinoa filling would also be great in small, crunchy taco shell cups and served as an appetizer.

NACHO PLATTER

Make an awesome nacho platter by spreading out 5 cups (250 g) tortilla chips and topping them with the Southwestern quinoa filling. Sprinkle cheddar cheese on top and bake for 15 minutes at 300°F/150°C/Gas Mark 2.

GINGER

Ginger has been used in Asian and Indian cuisine for centuries, and also has a long history of being used to relieve gastro-intestinal discomfort. This spicy root contains numerous anti-inflammatory and antioxidant compounds that benefit your health.

QUINOA-COATED FISH STICK SANDWICH

SERVES	4
PREP	15 minutes
COOK	15 minutes

YOU WILL NEED

1¼ cups (150 g) quinoa flakes

1 tablespoon finely chopped fresh flat-leaf parsley

zest of 1 lemon

14 oz. (400 g) firm white fish such as cod, haddock, hake, pollock, or coley

all-purpose flour, for coating

1 egg, beaten

4 multigrain rolls, cut in half

salt and black pepper

lemon wedges, lettuce, sliced tomatoes, and light mayonnaise, for serving

FREE FROM DAIRY

MAKE YOUR OWN DELICIOUS FISH STICKS FOR THE ULTIMATE SANDWICH. THIS RECIPE USES QUINOA FOR A CRUNCHY COATING.

1 Preheat the oven to 400°F/200°C/Gas Mark 6, and line a large cookie sheet with parchment.

2 Mix the quinoa flakes with the parsley and lemon zest, and season to taste with salt and black pepper.

3 Cut the fish fillets into thin sticks. Dip them in the flour then the egg and then coat them in the quinoa flake mixture. Chill for 10–15 minutes.

4 To cook the fish sticks, arrange them in one layer on the lined cookie sheet and bake for 15 minutes, until they are golden brown, turning them halfway through cooking.

5 For serving, place some lettuce and a sliced tomato on the bottom half of each bread roll, divide the fish sticks between the rolls, and then add a dollop of mayonnaise on top of the fish. Place the second half of the bread roll on top to make a sandwich.

VEGGIE AND QUINOA SUMMER ROLLS WITH CAJUN TAHINI SAUCE

SERVES	4
PREP	15 minutes
COOK	30 minutes

YOU WILL NEED

1 cup (240 ml) vegetable stock

⅓ cup (60 g) uncooked quinoa

olive oil, for grilling

4 oz. (115 g) portabella mushrooms, cut into 8 slices

1 medium zucchini, cut into 16 thin strips

1 large carrot, peeled and cut into 16 thin strips

16 snow peas, stems trimmed

8 sheets round rice paper

1 medium avocado, cut into cut into 8 thin slices

FOR THE CAJUN TAHINI SAUCE

¼ cup (60 ml) tahini

3 tablespoons water

1 tablespoon rice wine vinegar

1 tablespoon lime juice

1 teaspoon sriracha hot sauce

¼ teaspoon liquid smoke

pinch of salt

FREE FROM
DAIRY, GLUTEN & WHEAT

THIS RECIPE REVAMPS A STANDARD SUMMER ROLL BY INCORPORATING VEGETABLES, SEASONED QUINOA, AND A SMOKY DIPPING SAUCE.

1 Put the vegetable stock and quinoa in a saucepan, cover, and bring to a boil over medium heat. Reduce to medium-low heat and simmer for 20–25 minutes, or until all the liquid is gone and the quinoa is tender. Transfer the quinoa to a bowl and set aside to cool.

2 Bring a griddle up to medium heat, lightly coat with the olive oil, and spread the mushroom slices, zucchini, carrot, and snow peas over it. Cook for 3 minutes or until the vegetables are slightly charred, then flip over and cook for another 3 minutes. Set the vegetables aside to cool slightly.

3 Place warm water in a wide, shallow dish and gently submerge a sheet of rice paper in it for 4–5 seconds, lift it out, and drip dry.

4 Lay the rice paper flat and spoon 1½–2 tablespoons of quinoa just off-center in a rectangular shape. Place 1 slice of mushroom, 2 sticks of zucchini, 2 sticks of carrot, 2 snow peas, and 1 slice of avocado on top of the quinoa, working quickly.

5 Fold two sides of the rice paper in, width-wise, and roll the remainder up tightly, without tearing it. Repeat steps 3–5 for the remaining rolls.

6 For the sauce, whisk together all of the ingredients in a small bowl until smooth, and serve with the rolls.

QUINOA CRAB CAKES

SERVES	4
PREP	40 minutes
COOK	45 minutes

YOU WILL NEED

nonstick cooking spray,
for greasing

½ cup (100 g) uncooked
quinoa

1 cup (240 ml) fish or
vegetable stock

⅓ cup (180 g) cooked
crabmeat (canned or
fresh)

1 small red chili pepper,
finely diced

2 scallions, finely chopped

½ teaspoon garlic granules

½ teaspoon smoked paprika

zest of 1 lemon

cornstarch, to coat

salt and black pepper

lemon or lime wedges,
plain yogurt or
sour cream dressing,
and salad or fresh cilantro
leaves, for serving

FREE FROM
DAIRY, GLUTEN
& WHEAT

SPICY LITTLE QUINOA CRAB CAKES ARE EASY TO MAKE AND ARE PERFECT AS AN APPETIZER OR LIGHT LUNCH. SERVE THESE CRAB CAKES WITH A HOMEMADE TOMATO SAUCE AND SALAD LEAVES OR A LIGHT YOGURT OR SOUR CREAM DRESSING.

1 Preheat the oven to 400°F/200°C/Gas Mark 6. Coat a large cookie sheet with nonstick cooking spray.

2 Cook the quinoa in the stock for 15–20 minutes, or until all the liquid has been absorbed and the quinoa is fluffy. Remove from the heat and let cool for 10 minutes.

3 In a mixing bowl combine the quinoa with all of the other ingredients, except the cornstarch, and mix well. Season to taste with the salt and pepper. Cover the mixture and let it firm up in the refrigerator for 30–45 minutes.

4 Form the mixture into 12 little patties, dip them in the cornstarch to coat, and place the crab cakes on the cookie sheet. Bake for 30 minutes, or until they are crisp and golden brown. You may need to turn them over halfway through cooking so that they color evenly.

5 Serve immediately with wedges of lemon or lime, yogurt or dressing, a sprinkle of cilantro, and salad.

FISH CAKES
Fish can be used in place of the crab—use any firm white fish such as cod, haddock, pollock, or monkfish.

MAIN COURSES

QUINOA PIZZA WITH BLUE CHEESE AND EGGPLANT

SPROUTED QUINOA CHIRASHI SUSHI BOWL

SPROUTED QUINOA AND SALMON TEMAKI SUSHI

QUINOA BEAN BURGER WITH BASIL AÏOLI

SPICY PEANUT VEGGIE STEW WITH QUINOA DUMPLINGS

VEGETABLE PAELLA-STYLE QUINOA

CHIPOTLE SWEET POTATO QUINOA ENCHILADAS

BLACK BEAN, QUINOA, AND VEGETABLE CHILI

RISOTTO-STYLE QUINOA WITH CARAMELIZED ONIONS AND MUSHROOMS

SMOKY SPANISH QUINOA WITH CHICKEN AND CHORIZO

LAMB AND QUINOA MEATBALLS

Recipe on page 102

QUINOA PIZZA WITH BLUE CHEESE AND EGGPLANT

SERVES	2
PREP	20 minutes
COOK	45 minutes

THIS DELICIOUS GLUTEN-FREE PIZZA IS HEALTHY AND LOADED WITH TRUSTY CHEESE, VEGETABLES, AND HERBS. ONCE THE CRUST IS MADE YOU CAN ADD ANY TOPPINGS YOU LIKE.

YOU WILL NEED

1 eggplant, cut into thin strips

extra-virgin olive oil, for frying

½ can (7 oz./200 g) diced tomatoes

1 teaspoon dried oregano

½ cup (75 g) crumbled blue cheese

salad, for serving

FOR THE CRUST

¾ cup (150 g) uncooked quinoa, soaked for 8 hours or overnight, and drained

¼ cup (60 ml) water

1 egg

1 teaspoon baking powder

½ teaspoon sea salt

2 tablespoons olive oil

FREE FROM
GLUTEN & WHEAT

1 Preheat the oven to 425°F/220°C/Gas Mark 7 and line a 9-inch (23-cm) tart or cake pan with parchment.

2 Put all of the pizza crust ingredients in a blender and blend on high until the mixture resembles a thick pancake batter.

3 Pour the crust batter into the prepared pan and bake for 30 minutes, until the crust is crisp and set firm. Ease the crust out of the pan and put it on a lined pizza tray.

4 While the crust is cooking, fry the eggplant strips in a little olive oil until soft and just charred on the edges.

5 To assemble the pizza, spoon the tomatoes over the crust, sprinkle with oregano, and then arrange the cooked eggplant strips over the top. Sprinkle on the blue cheese and bake for 10–15 minutes, until the cheese has melted and the topping is hot.

6 Serve immediately with salad.

TIME SAVING TIP: The crust batter can be frozen, so make extra and freeze the mixture you don't use for fast future meals.

QUINOA PIZZA VARIATIONS
THERE'S NO NEED TO SERVE TAKEOUT—THIS BASIC QUINOA PIZZA DOUGH IS A CROWD-PLEASING AND INVALUABLE RECIPE FOR YOUR GLUTEN-FREE KITCHEN.

HAWAIIAN CHEESY QUINOA PIZZA

Add I cup (IOO g) shredded cheddar cheese to the crust and bake as in the main recipe on page 82. When the crust is cooked, add the toppings in the following order: ½ can (7 oz./200 g) diced tomatoes; ½ teaspoon dried oregano; ⅔ cup (100 g) chopped cooked ham; 4 canned pineapple rings, drained and diced; ¾ cup (75 g) shredded mozzarella cheese. Bake in a 425°F/220°C/Gas Mark 7 oven for IO minutes, or until the cheese has melted and is bubbling. Serve the pizza with salad.

INDIVIDUAL MARGHERITA QUINOA PIZZAS

Make the quinoa crust batter as described on page 82, but pour the batter into 2 × 4-hole Yorkshire pudding pans, or into an 8-hole shallow patty pan. Bake for 20 minutes, until the crusts have set and are crisp. Let cool for 5 minutes and then ease the crusts out of the pans gently and place them on a greased cookie sheet. Add the toppings in the following order: ½ can (7 oz./200 g) diced tomatoes mixed with I ½ teaspoons dried oregano, I tablespoon tomato paste, and I teaspoon sugar, then 5 oz. (150 g) mozzarella cheese, torn into small pieces. Bake the individual pizzas for about 5 minutes, until the sauce is hot and the cheese has melted. Serve warm or cold with salad and olives.

SPICY MEAT FEAST QUINOA PARTY PIZZA

This meaty and spicy version of the pizza is rectangular and can be served cut into small squares, which makes it perfect finger food. Make the crust as described on page 82, but spoon it into a well-greased and lined rectangular dish or tray, about 9 × 5 inches (22 x 12 cm). Bake until crispy. Add the toppings in the following order: ½ can (7 oz./200 g) diced tomatoes mixed with I teaspoon of dried chili powder, I tablespoon tomato paste, and I teaspoon of sugar; I ½ oz. (50 g) sliced peppered salami; I ½ oz. (50 g) diced cooked ham; I ½ oz. (50 g) diced Spanish chorizo; I teaspoon capers, drained; and I cup (100 g) shredded smoked cheddar cheese. Bake for IO–I5 minutes, until the topping is cooked and the cheese has melted. Let the pizza cool for 5 minutes before cutting into squares and serving.

TOMATOES

Tomatoes, whether fresh or canned, count toward your five-a-day and are packed with vitamins including C, B6, and E. They also contain folic acid, which is essential for bone development and cell regrowth. Tomatoes can be eaten raw or cooked and are the basis of many popular family recipes. Unless you need a smooth paste or sauce, there is no need to discard the skin or the seeds.

SPROUTED QUINOA CHIRASHI SUSHI BOWL

MAKES	1
PREP	15 minutes, plus sprouting
COOK	5 minutes

YOU WILL NEED

2 cups (200 g) sprouted quinoa

2 tablespoons rice wine vinegar

2 tablespoons sesame seeds

1 egg

½ tablespoon sugar

1 teaspoon mirin

canola or sunflower oil for the skillet or omelet pan

2 ½ oz. (70 g) snow peas

1 ½-in. (3½-cm) chunk of cucumber, sliced

3 ½ oz. (100 g) fresh sushi-grade tuna, sliced

3 ½ oz. (100 g) fresh sushi-grade salmon, sliced

small handful of mustard cress

pickled ginger and tamari or gluten-free soy sauce, for serving

FREE FROM
DAIRY, GLUTEN & WHEAT

CHIRASHI SUSHI MEANS "SCATTERED SUSHI" AND IT'S THE PERFECT SOLUTION FOR LAZY FANS OF THE DELICATE ART OF SUSHI MAKING. SPROUTED QUINOA MAKES A LIGHT ALTERNATIVE TO SUSHI RICE.

1 Put the sprouted quinoa in a bowl. Add the rice wine vinegar and sesame seeds, and stir together. Spoon the quinoa mixture into your serving bowl.

2 Beat the egg with the sugar and mirin. Warm a little oil in a small skillet or omelet pan over low heat. Pour in the omelet mixture. Swirl the skillet so the bottom is evenly coated, and let the egg cook until it's almost set in the middle. Loosen the edges with a spatula, flip the omelet over, and cook for 10−20 seconds. Slide it out of the skillet. Let the omelet cool for a few minutes, then roll it up and slice it.

3 While the omelet is cooking, fill a saucepan with water and bring it to a boil. Add the snow peas. Simmer without a lid for 2 minutes, to just blanch the peas. Drain and rinse them under cold water.

4 Top the quinoa with the sliced omelet, snow peas, cucumber, tuna, and salmon. Serve topped with mustard cress, with pickled ginger and tamari or soy sauce on the side.

ABOUT SPROUTS: For tips on sprouting quinoa, turn to page 91.

CHIRASHI BOWL VARIATIONS

ONCE YOU'VE GOT YOUR BOWL OF SEASONED SPROUTED QUINOA, YOU CAN MIX AND MATCH YOUR FAVORITE TRADITIONAL—AND NOT-SO-TRADITIONAL—SUSHI TOPPINGS. TRY THE RECIPES BELOW FOR A BIT OF VARIATION, OR WHY NOT INVENT YOUR OWN COMBINATIONS?

RAW VEGAN CHIRASHI BOWL

Following the main recipe on page 86, season the sprouted quinoa with the vinegar and sesame seeds then top it with a mixture of sliced avocado, carrot, cucumber, red bell pepper, red onion, corn kernels, and shredded nori. Dress the sushi bowl with a squeeze of lemon juice and serve with some pickled ginger, soy sauce, and wasabi.

SMOKED SALMON AND PICKLED CUCUMBER CHIRASHI BOWL

Slice half a cucumber as thinly as possible. Put it in a bowl with ¼ cup (60 ml) rice wine vinegar, 2 tablespoons sugar, and ½ tablespoon kosher salt. Let sit for 30 minutes while you make the sweet omelet per the main recipe. Stir 2 tablespoons of the cucumber brine into the sprouted quinoa with the sesame seeds. Top the quinoa with the pickled cucumber, 4 oz. (115 g) smoked salmon, a couple of cooked shrimp, the sliced omelet, and some shiso, sorrel, or baby spinach leaves.

TOFU, GREEN BEAN, AND TOMATO CHIRASHI

Pat a 7-oz. (200-g) block of tofu dry with paper towel and slice it into small chunks. Sprinkle the tofu with a little salt and I tablespoon cornstarch. Turn it over a few times to coat it in the cornstarch. Warm a splash of sunflower or canola oil in a skillet. Add the tofu and fry for 2 minutes, until the tofu doesn't stick to the skillet. Flip it over and fry until it's golden on both sides. Put it in a bowl. Mix together I tablespoon mirin and tablespoon light soy sauce and pour it over the tofu. Simmer 7 oz. (200 g) green beans for 2–3 minutes, until just tender. Drain. Divide the sprouted quinoa between two serving bowls, then top with the tofu, green beans, 6 halved baby plum tomatoes per person, and a couple of shredded scallions. Drizzle the sauce from the tofu over the chirashi for serving.

SPROUTED QUINOA AND SALMON TEMAKI SUSHI

MAKES	2
PREP	10 minutes, plus sprouting
COOK	2 minutes

YOU WILL NEED

1 cup (100 g) sprouted quinoa

1 tablespoon rice wine vinegar

1 tablespoon sesame seeds

1 sheet of nori

2 sticks cucumber

1 tablespoon shredded daikon

2 oz. (60 g) sushi-grade salmon, sliced into sticks

salt and black pepper

pickled ginger and tamari or gluten-free soy sauce, for serving

(pictured on page 90)

FREE FROM
DAIRY, GLUTEN & WHEAT

TEMAKI HAND ROLLS ARE THE EASIEST KIND OF SUSHI TO MAKE. YOU JUST NEED A SHEET OF NORI, SOME SPROUTED QUINOA, AND A FEW STRIPS OF FISH, VEG, OR OMELET. NO NEED FOR YEARS OF STUDY, NO SPECIAL TOOLS—YOU CAN JUST GET ROLLING.

1 Place the sprouted quinoa in a bowl. Stir in the rice wine vinegar with a pinch of salt until thoroughly combined.

2 Pour the sesame seeds into a dry skillet. Toast over low heat for 1–2 minutes, until the sesame seeds are golden. Keep stirring while they toast so they don't burn. Stir them into the quinoa.

3 Slice the sheet of nori in half so you have two rectangles. Make sure your hands are dry, and hold the end of one sheet in your left hand if you're right-handed, the right if you're left-handed. Heap half of the quinoa onto the nori and flatten it with the back of a spoon.

4 Top the quinoa with 1 stick of cucumber and half the shredded daikon, placed on the quinoa at a diagonal, pointing toward the empty end of the nori. Lay a few strips of salmon on top.

5 Roll the nori around the sprouted quinoa tightly on the diagonal to make a cone-shaped roll.

6 Repeat with the other sheet of nori and fillings to make 2 rolls. Serve with pickled ginger and tamari or soy sauce.

TEMAKI ROLL VARIATIONS

YOU CAN PUT ALMOST ANYTHING IN A TEMAKI HAND ROLL—THINK OF IT LIKE A SANDWICH AND MIX AND MATCH FILLINGS UNTIL YOU GET THE PERFECT TEMAKI ROLL.

NEED SOME INSPIRATION? TRY SOME OF THESE COMBINATIONS

- Strips of smoked salmon and sliced avocado
- Flaked smoked mackerel and sliced cooked beet
- Shredded cooked chicken and sliced mango
- Strips of sweet omelet (see page 86), shredded scallions, and slices of red bell pepper
- Strips of grilled bell pepper, rare steak, and arugula
- Blanched asparagus spears and smoked trout
- Strips of raw tuna, shredded scallions, and wasabi mayonnaise
- Sliced, broiled portabella mushrooms, cooked beets, and spinach
- Fried tofu steaks, cucumber, and sliced radishes
- Diced shrimp combined with mayo, sriracha, and shredded scallions.

Why not try your favorite sashimi flavors in a temaki roll.

HOW TO SPROUT QUINOA

Sprouting is the traditional practice of germinating seeds, nuts, grains, and legumes under controlled conditions to increase their nutritional content and make them more easily digestible.

Sprouted quinoa is easy to make and is a delicious addition to salads, sandwiches, and other dishes. To make about 2 cups (200 g) of sprouted quinoa:

- Rinse I cup (200 g) of quinoa under running water until the water turns clear.

- Place the rinsed quinoa in a I-quart (2 l) Mason jar and fill it with cold filtered water. Let sit for about 6 hours.

- Drain the water and put on a sprouting lid. (A sprouting lid is a piece of fine mesh that replaces the regular lid insert. It is inexpensive and easy to find online.) Place the jar upside down in a bowl to catch drips.

- A few times a day, rinse the sprouts with plenty of clean water and place the jar back in the bowl to drain. In a day or two, you should see lots of little sprouts.

- Spread the sprouts on a clean plate and cover with paper towels. Let the sprouts dry out. Then store in an airtight container in the refrigerator for up to 2 weeks.

QUINOA BEAN BURGER WITH BASIL AÏOLI

SERVES	6
PREP	20 minutes
COOK	40 minutes

YOU WILL NEED

1 tablespoon freshly ground flaxseed

1 can (14 oz./400 g) cannellini beans, drained, rinsed, and mashed

1 cup (180 g) cooked quinoa

½ cup (125 g) white potatoes, roasted and mashed

¼ cup (15 g) nutritional yeast

½ red onion, finely diced

large handful of fresh basil, minced

2 garlic cloves, minced

2 tablespoons gluten-free all-purpose flour, plus extra for forming the burgers

⅓ cup (80 ml) vegan mayonnaise

2 tablespoons basil pesto

salt and black pepper

gluten-free buns and lettuce, for serving

FREE FROM
DAIRY, GLUTEN
& WHEAT

THIS SAVORY BURGER IS PACKED WITH FRESH HERBS AND THE FLAVORS OF SUMMER.

1 Preheat the oven to 350°F/180°C/Gas Mark 4.

2 Combine the flaxseed with 3 tablespoons of warm water. Set aside to gel. (This process is often called making a flax "egg.")

3 Combine the beans, quinoa, potatoes, nutritional yeast, onion, basil, and garlic in a large bowl, and stir or use your hands to incorporate the ingredients. Add the flour and the flaxseed gel, and combine completely. Using flour (flour your hands and have a plate of flour to work with), form patties 3½ inches (9 cm) round and ½ inch (1.5 cm) thick (or slightly smaller if you prefer).

4 Transfer the burgers to a cookie sheet and bake for 40 minutes, flipping the burgers after 20 minutes.

5 To make the basil aïoli, put the vegan mayonnaise in a bowl with the basil pesto and stir until combined.

6 Serve the burgers with fresh buns, lettuce, and a bowl of the aïoli on the side.

A LIGHTER OPTION: Instead of a bun, try serving the burgers wrapped in lettuce leaves for a low-carb option.

QUINOA BURGER VARIATIONS

MIX UP YOUR BEAN BURGERS BY STACKING THEM WITH COLORFUL VEGGIES, TRYING DIFFERENT BEANS AND ROOTS, OR PAIRING COOL, TANGY LEMON AÏOLI WITH HEARTY LENTILS. THE BEST WAY TO FINISH THE BLACK-BEAN BUTTERNUT BURGER IS ON THE OUTDOOR GRILL—CRISPY GOODNESS GALORE!

BLACK-BEAN BUTTERNUT BURGER

Omit the basil, swap the cannellini beans for black beans, and replace the mashed potatoes with roasted, mashed butternut squash per the main recipe on page 92. This burger tastes great with chipotle aïoli. To make it, combine 1/3 cup (80 ml) vegan mayonnaise with 1 canned chipotle pepper in adobo, very finely chopped.

RAINBOW STACK BURGERS

Omit the basil in the main recipe. Garnish the burger with slices of tomato, orange bell pepper, avocado, and red onion. Spread the bun with yellow mustard and fry sauce (1/3 cup/80 ml vegan mayonnaise combined with 3 tablespoons of tomato ketchup).

HEARTY LEMON LENTIL BURGERS

Omit the basil in the main recipe. Reduce the quantity of cooked quinoa to ¾ cup (135 g). Replace the cannellini beans with 1½ cups cooked lentils, and the juice and zest of 1 lemon, reserving 1 tablespoon of the juice. To make the lemon aïoli, combine 1/3 cup (80 ml) vegan mayonnaise with the reserved tablespoon of lemon juice.

BUTTERNUT SQUASH

The butternut is a favorite among the succulent squash fruits, and the status is well earned. Butternut squash is rich in antioxidants, vitamins, phytonutrients, and minerals. It contains a significant amount of fiber and is naturally low in fat. Brightly colored and vibrantly flavored, butternut squash is incredibly versatile, which makes it great for savory and sweet options. Try it in sweet quick breads, warming soups, layered into a lovely lasagna, or tucked into a veggie burger.

SPICY PEANUT VEGGIE STEW WITH QUINOA DUMPLINGS

SERVES	6–8
PREP	20 minutes
COOK	50 minutes

YOU WILL NEED

2 tablespoons olive oil

1 onion, chopped

1–2 garlic cloves, minced

3 large carrots, scrubbed and diced

3 stalks celery, diced

2 cans (28 oz./800 g) diced tomatoes

2 cups (20 g) sliced cremini mushrooms

1 red bell pepper, seeded and diced

1 jalapeño, seeded and diced

8 cups (2 l) vegetable stock

⅔ cup (160 g) peanut butter

2 teaspoons red pepper flakes (adjust according to heat preference)

salt and black pepper

FREE FROM
DAIRY, GLUTEN & WHEAT

THIS HEARTY, FLAVOR-PACKED STEW INCLUDES FLUFFY QUINOA DUMPLINGS AND IS A COMFORT ON COLDER NIGHTS.

1 Heat the olive oil in a saucepan over medium heat, and sauté the onion, garlic, carrots and celery until the onion is translucent. Add the tomatoes, mushrooms, pepper, jalapeño, stock, peanut butter, and red pepper flakes to taste, and let the stew mixture simmer for 20–30 minutes, stirring occasionally, until the vegetables have softened but have some bite. Add salt and black pepper to taste.

2 To make the dumplings, sift together the flours, baking powder, onion powder, and salt. Add the soda water and olive oil, stirring twice around the bowl. Add the quinoa and stir until just combined; do not overstir—the batter can be just slightly "together."

3 Increase the heat to high, and bring the stew to a boil. Drop the dumpling dough in small spoonfuls into the stew, and cook for 10 minutes. Cover and steam for another 8–10 minutes, until the dumplings are tender. Once the dumplings are fully cooked and the stew is removed from the heat, do not cover the pot, as the dumplings will continue to steam and will overcook.

FOR THE DUMPLINGS

¾ cup (120 g) rice flour
¾ cup (90 g) all-purpose flour
I tablespoon baking powder
I tablespoon onion powder
I teaspoon salt
¾ cup (180 ml) soda water
1½ tablespoons olive oil
½ cup (90 g) cooked quinoa

VEGETABLE PAELLA-STYLE QUINOA

SERVES	4
PREP	20 minutes
COOK	35 minutes, plus resting

YOU WILL NEED

½ teaspoon saffron threads

¼ cup (60 ml) hot water

⅓ cup (80 ml) olive oil

1 onion, finely diced

3 fresh tomatoes, seeded and chopped

4 garlic cloves

2 teaspoons smoked paprika

1 teaspoon fine sea salt (less if the stock is salty)

4 cups (1 l) vegetable stock

1 dried bay leaf

1½ cups (300 g) uncooked quinoa

1 cup (150 g) frozen artichoke quarters, defrosted

1 cup (150 g) peas, fresh or frozen

1 cup (150 g) cut green beans, fresh or frozen

3 piquillo peppers, drained and sliced

black pepper

lemon wedges, for serving

FREE FROM
DAIRY, GLUTEN & WHEAT

SPANISH PAELLA IS RENOWNED FOR THE DELICIOUS FLAVOR COMBINATION OF SMOKY PAPRIKA WITH FRAGRANT SAFFRON. THIS VEGETARIAN VERSION RETAINS THE AROMATICS OF THE TRADITIONAL RECIPE, BUT HAS THE ADDED TEXTURE OF QUINOA.

1 Crumble the saffron threads into a small bowl and pour over the hot water. Let it sit for 10 minutes to make saffron-flavored liquid.

2 Heat the olive oil over medium-high heat in a cast-iron skillet. Add the onion, tomato, garlic, paprika, and ½ teaspoon salt and cook, stirring from time to time, until the onion is softened and lightly translucent. This should take about 10 minutes.

3 Add the stock, saffron and soaking liquid, bay leaf, remaining ½ teaspoon salt, and a few grinds of black pepper, stir and bring to a boil over high heat. Sprinkle in the quinoa and arrange evenly across the surface of the skillet. Reduce the heat as necessary to simmer until most of the liquid has been absorbed, about 15 minutes. Do not stir. If the burner does not heat the skillet evenly, rotate the skillet every once in a while to compensate, so that the mixture is evenly heated.

4 Scatter the artichokes, peas, green beans, and peppers evenly throughout the skillet, pressing down gently to submerge some of the vegetables beneath the surface. Continue simmering, without stirring, until all of the liquid is absorbed, about 7 minutes more. Then turn up the heat all the way and cook undisturbed for 3 minutes. At this stage you should hear the paella crackling gently. Let the skillet sit off the heat for 10 minutes before serving.

PAELLA-STYLE QUINOA VARIATIONS

THIS DISH IS BURSTING WITH FLAVOR IN ITS VEGAN INCARNATION, BUT IF YOU LIKE SEAFOOD, YOU CAN'T BEAT THE ALTERNATIVE VERSION WITH SHRIMP AND MUSSELS. QUINOA PAIRS BEAUTIFULLY WITH THE BRINY FLAVORS OF THE SEA.

SEAFOOD PAELLA

Peel and de-vein 1 lb. (450 g) extra-large shrimp and season with salt. When the oil is heated, cook the shrimp for about 2 minutes per side, until just barely cooked through. Transfer to a plate. Bring a small amount of water to a boil in a saucepan with a lid. Add 16 cleaned mussels and steam until they open, discarding any that don't open. To cook the quinoa, replace the vegetable stock with seafood stock and follow the main recipe on page 98. Omit the artichokes. Arrange the seafood over the cooked paella.

PUT AN EGG ON IT!

This variation might not pass a Spanish authenticity test, but smoked paprika is a natural companion to both fried eggs and paella, and here it ties together the two elements perfectly. Fry an egg in a generous glug of olive oil until crispy around the edges, and sprinkle with a little salt and smoked paprika. To get crispy edges without overcooking, don't flip the egg. Instead, flick a few drops of water into the skillet halfway through cooking and quickly place a lid on top. The steam will gently cook the top of the egg while the bottom crisps over direct heat. Follow the main recipe to make the paella.

PAELLA-STYLE QUINOA WITH CHICKPEAS AND CHORIZO

Spanish chorizo is a dried and cured sausage (not to be confused with Mexican chorizo). It is flavored with smoked paprika and goes beautifully with paella, as well as with chickpeas. You can use vegan chorizo-style sausage as an alternative. To make this variation, slice a Spanish chorizo link and brown the pieces on both sides in 2 tablespoons of the olive oil before adding the remaining oil, onion, tomato, and other ingredients per the main recipe. When brown, remove to a paper towel-lined plate and set aside. Add 1 can (14 oz./400 g) chickpeas and the browned sausage pieces along with the peas, green beans, and peppers. Omit the artichokes.

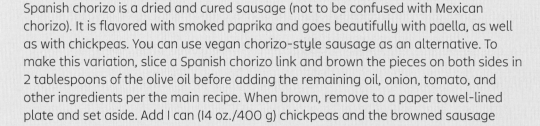

SAFFRON

Saffron is a wonderfully aromatic spice that lends both deep flavor and vibrant color to food. It has been revered in numerous cultures—from India to Rome—since ancient times. You'll find it sold in very small packages containing just a pinch of its fragile threads. Each thread is one stamen of a crocus flower (and flowers contain only 3 stamen each). The threads are carefully harvested by hand in a laborious process, which is one reason why saffron is among the most expensive spices in the world. Luckily a little goes a long way, so you can enjoy saffron in paella and other dishes without breaking the bank.

CHIPOTLE SWEET POTATO QUINOA ENCHILADAS

MAKES	4
PREP	25 minutes
COOK	1 hour 15 minutes

YOU WILL NEED

2 large sweet potatoes, cut into cubes

2 tablespoons olive oil

salt and black pepper

1 cup (200 g) uncooked quinoa

1 cup (240 ml) tomato juice (or water or stock)

2–3 canned chipotle peppers in adobo, chopped

4 large whole-wheat tortillas

2 cups (350 g) fresh corn (from 3–4 cobs)

1 can (14 oz./400 g) black beans

½ cup (120 g) nondairy sour cream

3 tablespoons almond milk

3 plum tomatoes, seeded and diced, for garnish

1 avocado, peeled, pitted, and diced, for garnish

handful chopped fresh cilantro, for garnish

YOU CAN ADJUST THE QUANTITY OF CHIPOTLE PEPPERS IN THIS RECIPE TO SUIT YOUR TASTE FOR SPICE. TOPPING WITH COOL AVOCADO IS A NICE BALANCE.

1 Preheat the oven to 350°F/180°C/Gas Mark 4. Prepare a cookie sheet by lining it with parchment.

2 Arrange the sweet potato in a single layer on the cookie sheet, drizzle with the olive oil, and season with salt and black pepper. Roast for 25 minutes, until the potato is tender.

3 In a medium pot over high heat, bring the quinoa, tomato juice, and ½ cup (120 ml) of water to a rolling boil. Reduce to a simmer, cover, and cook the mixture for 18–20 minutes, until all liquid is absorbed. Stir in the chipotle peppers.

4 In a dry skillet over low heat (or for a few seconds in the microwave), warm the tortillas individually before filling. Spoon 3–4 tablespoons of cooked quinoa down the middle of each tortilla. Top with a quarter of the corn, black beans, and roasted potato. Roll, and place open side down in an 8 × 8-inch (20 × 20-cm) baking dish. Repeat with the remaining tortillas until the dish is full of enchiladas.

5 Cover with aluminum foil and bake for 30 minutes. Remove the foil and continue cooking for another 5–7 minutes.

6 Thin the sour cream with the almond milk and drizzle over the enchiladas. Scatter with the diced tomatoes and avocado, and top with the fresh cilantro, for serving.

BLACK BEAN, QUINOA, AND VEGETABLE CHILI

SERVES	8
PREP	10 minutes
COOK	45 minutes

YOU WILL NEED

2 tablespoons olive oil

1 red onion, diced

1 green bell pepper, diced

4 garlic cloves, minced

2 tablespoons tomato paste

1 tablespoon chili powder

1 teaspoon smoked paprika

1 teaspoon ground cumin

½ teaspoon dried oregano

3 cups (720 ml) good
    vegetable stock

1 cup (200 g) uncooked red
    quinoa

1 sweet potato, peeled and
    cut into ½-in. (1.5 cm)
    dice

2 cans (28 oz./800 g) black
    beans, drained and rinsed

2 cans (28 oz./800 g) diced
    tomatoes

2 cups (350 g) corn kernels
    (thawed if frozen)

salt

½ cup (30 g) chopped fresh
    cilantro

diced avocado, shredded
    cheese, sour cream, and
    lime wedges, for serving

**FREE FROM
GLUTEN & WHEAT**

THIS RECIPE MAKES A BIG BATCH OF HEARTY, DEEPLY FLAVORED CHILI. IT ONLY IMPROVES THE FOLLOWING DAY, SO IT'S EQUALLY GOOD FOR MAKING IN ADVANCE OF A PARTY, FOR A COUPLE OF FAMILY DINNERS, OR FOR A WEEK'S WORTH OF LUNCHES.

1 In a medium pot, heat the olive oil over medium-high heat. Add the onion and pepper and a sprinkle of salt and cook, stirring from time to time until softened, about 5 minutes. Add the garlic, tomato paste, chili powder, smoked paprika, cumin, and oregano and cook, stirring frequently, about 2 minutes more.

2 Add the stock and the remaining salt, the quinoa, and the sweet potato. Raise the heat to high, bring to a boil, then cover and reduce the heat; simmer for 20 minutes.

3 Add the beans, tomatoes, and corn and simmer for 15 minutes more. Uncover for the last 5 minutes to reduce the sauce a bit. Taste and adjust for salt. Stir in the cilantro.

4 Ladle the chili into bowls and serve with the diced avocado, cheese, sour cream, and lime wedges.

RISOTTO-STYLE QUINOA WITH CARAMELIZED ONIONS AND MUSHROOMS

SERVES	4
PREP	20 minutes
COOK	1 hour 30 minutes, plus resting

YOU WILL NEED

8 dried shiitake mushrooms

1 teaspoon herbes de Provence

1 dried bay leaf

4 cups (1 l) vegetable stock

1 teaspoon fine sea salt, if needed

3 tablespoons butter

3 tablespoons olive oil

3 onions, peeled, halved, and sliced thinly from tip to root

½ cup (120 ml) dry white wine

8 oz. (225 g) shiitake mushrooms, stems removed and sliced

8 oz. (225 g) cremini mushrooms, sliced

2 teaspoons soy sauce

(continued)

THIS RECIPE PACKS THE FLAVOR PUNCH OF A REAL ITALIAN RISOTTO DISH, SATISFYING YOUR CRAVING FOR CREAMY, COMFORTING GOODNESS.

1 Place the dried shiitakes, herbes de Provence, and bay leaf in a small pot and pour in the stock. If the stock is unsalted, add ¾ teaspoon of fine sea salt. Bring the mixture to a boil, then cover and simmer for 5 minutes. Remove from the heat and let the mixture steep while you caramelize the onions, and longer if you have the time—several hours or overnight results in the best flavor.

2 In a 12-inch (30 cm) skillet, heat I tablespoon of the butter and I tablespoon of the olive oil over medium to medium-low heat. When melted, add the onions. Cook, undisturbed, for 10 minutes—you want to hear a gentle sizzle—then stir gently, scraping up any brown bits on the bottom of the skillet, and add ¼ teaspoon of salt. Continue cooking on medium to medium-low heat, stirring occasionally, for 35–50 minutes more, until the onions are substantially reduced in volume, soft but not mushy, and beautifully browned. Don't be tempted to raise the heat even if it's hard to be patient—but do lower it slightly if necessary to prevent burning. Deglaze the skillet with I tablespoon of the wine, then raise the heat and cook for another minute until the wine has evaporated. Place the onions in a small bowl.

(continued)

1 ½ cups (300 g) uncooked
    quinoa

1 teaspoon chopped fresh
    thyme leaves

½ cup (50 g) shredded
    vegetarian Parmesan
    cheese, plus extra for
    serving

¼ cup (15 g) finely chopped
    fresh flat-leaf parsley

black pepper

3 In the same skillet, melt 1 tablespoon of butter with 1 tablespoon of the olive oil over medium-high heat. Add the shiitakes, creminis, and soy sauce. Simmer undisturbed for 2–3 minutes, then stir frequently while cooking until the mushrooms have released and reabsorbed any juices as well as browning nicely. They should substantially decrease in volume, 5–10 minutes. Deglaze the skillet with 1 tablespoon of wine. Set the mushrooms aside in a small bowl.

4 In the same skillet, melt the remaining tablespoon of butter with the remaining tablespoon of olive oil over medium-high heat. Add the quinoa and cook, stirring constantly, until lightly fragrant, 2–3 minutes. Add the remaining wine and cook, stirring, until absorbed. Raise the heat to high, add the thyme, and ladle in the stock one or two ladles at a time, leaving the dried mushrooms and bay leaf in the pot to discard later. Cook until the stock is nearly absorbed before adding more. Stir very frequently. This process will take about 15 minutes. When the last of the broth is almost absorbed, turn off the heat and cover the skillet. Let the risotto sit for 10 minutes to allow it to thicken.

5 Stir in the onions, mushrooms, Parmesan, parsley, and a few good grinds of black pepper. Serve the risotto in bowls with extra fresh shredded Parmesan cheese to pass around.

ADVANCE PLANNING: Caramelizing the onions is a bit time-consuming, but you can do it up to a few days in advance.

QUINOA-STYLE RISOTTO VARIATIONS

QUINOA RISOTTO IS JUST AS ADAPTABLE AS TRADITIONAL RISOTTO IN TERMS OF BOTH FLAVOR AND FORMAT. HERE ARE SOME SUGGESTIONS TO GET YOU STARTED, BUT FEEL FREE TO RIFF ON THIS THEME WITH WHATEVER SEASONAL INGREDIENTS YOU HAVE AVAILABLE.

QUICK RISOTTO

For a much quicker risotto with a similar flavor profile, omit the caramelized onions. Dice 1 onion and sauté until it is soft and translucent (this process should take about 7 minutes). Add the quinoa and proceed as directed in the main recipe.

SPRINGY RISOTTO

Omit the fresh and dried mushrooms, soy sauce, and thyme per the main recipe. Add 1 cup (150 g) peas; 1 bunch thin-stemmed asparagus, cut into 1-inch (2.5 cm) lengths; and 2 tablespoons minced fresh tarragon 5 minutes before the end of cooking. If desired, stir in 4 oz. (115 g) crumbled fresh goat cheese along with the Parmesan.

RISOTTO CAKES

If you have leftovers, beat 1 egg in a medium bowl, scoop in up to 2 cups (360 g) of leftover risotto-style quinoa, and mix well. On a plate, sprinkle 1 cup (60 g) panko or dry breadcrumbs. Form the risotto mixture into small patties and dredge in the breadcrumbs to coat. Heat a thin layer of oil in a skillet over medium-high heat and cook the patties in batches until golden brown on each side and heated through.

SMOKY SPANISH QUINOA WITH CHICKEN AND CHORIZO

SERVES	2
PREP	15 minutes
COOK	30–35 minutes

YOU WILL NEED

pinch of saffron threads

1 cup (240 ml) hot chicken stock

extra-virgin olive oil, for frying

2 skinless, boneless chicken breasts, chopped

2½ oz (70 g) Spanish chorizo, skinned and diced

1 onion, finely chopped

1 red bell pepper, roughly chopped

1 green bell pepper, roughly chopped

1 garlic clove, minced

2 teaspoons smoked paprika

½ cup (100 g) uncooked quinoa

salt and black pepper

fresh flat-leaf parsley and lemon wedges, for serving

FREE FROM
DAIRY, GLUTEN & WHEAT

FLAVORED WITH SAFFRON, GARLIC, AND PAPRIKA, PAELLA IS ONE OF THOSE GREAT DISHES THAT CAN ALWAYS BE ADAPTED. QUINOA IS USED HERE INSTEAD OF RICE, WITH CHICKEN AND CHORIZO TO MAKE IT A REALLY HEARTY DISH.

1 Add a pinch of saffron threads to the hot chicken stock and let them soak for a few minutes until they start to release their color. Give the stock a stir to thoroughly disperse the flavor.

2 Warm a splash of olive oil in a deep skillet. Add the chicken. Fry over medium heat for 5 minutes, until the chicken is browned all over. Stir every so often so it gets an even color. Lift out of the skillet with a slotted spoon or spatula, and put it on a plate.

3 Add the chorizo to the skillet. Stir and fry for 2 minutes until it has browned a little and released plenty of red, spicy oils.

4 Add the onion and peppers to the skillet. Season with salt and black pepper. Cook and stir for 5 minutes, until the vegetables are starting to soften. Stir in the garlic and smoked paprika.

5 Add the chicken along with any juices from the plate, then stir in the quinoa. Pour in the saffron chicken stock and cover.

6 Bring the quinoa mixture to a boil, then turn the heat down. Gently simmer for 10–15 minutes, until the stock has been absorbed and the quinoa is tender.

7 Taste and adjust the seasoning according to taste. Serve scattered with sprigs of flat-leaf parsley and lemon wedges for squeezing.

SMOKY SPANISH QUINOA WITH SEAFOOD AND CHORIZO

Swap the diced chicken for 2 skinned and chopped fillets of firm white fish such as cod, haddock, whiting, hake, or pollock. Don't fry it at the beginning, but add once most of the stock has been absorbed so it cooks for 5–8 minutes. You can also add a handful of cleaned mussels or clams to the skillet with the fish, if you like. The fish should be white and opaque and the shellfish should be open when the quinoa is ready (discard any shells that don't open.)

LAMB AND QUINOA MEATBALLS

SERVES	4
PREP	15 minutes, plus chilling
COOK	1 hour

THIS DISH HAS A MIDDLE EASTERN TWIST, WITH SWEET AND SHARP POMEGRANATE MOLASSES IN THE SAUCE. QUINOA IS ADDED TO THE MEATBALL MIXTURE TO KEEP IT LIGHT AND MOIST.

YOU WILL NEED

¼ cup (50 g) uncooked quinoa

½ cup (120 ml) water

9 oz. (250 g) ground lamb

2 garlic cloves, minced

1 red chili pepper, minced

1 small onion, finely chopped

handful of fresh flat-leaf parsley, finely chopped

1 tablespoon tahini

pinch of cayenne pepper

olive oil, for frying

salt and black pepper

FOR THE TOMATO SAUCE

1 onion, finely chopped

1 long red bell pepper, finely chopped

2 garlic cloves, minced

1 teaspoon sumac

1 can (14 oz./400 g) diced tomatoes

1 tablespoon pomegranate molasses

salt and black pepper

cooked quinoa and fresh cilantro, for serving

FREE FROM
DAIRY, GLUTEN & WHEAT

1 Put the quinoa in a saucepan with the water. Cover, bring to a boil, then turn the heat down and gently simmer for 10–15 minutes, or until all the water has been absorbed and the quinoa is tender and fluffy. If it looks like it's getting too dry while it cooks, add a splash more water. Drain well.

2 Transfer the cooked quinoa to a bowl. Add the lamb, garlic, chili, onion, parsley leaves and stalks, and tahini. Season with a pinch of cayenne and salt and black pepper. Knead everything together for a few minutes until well mixed.

3 Pull a lump off the meatball mixture and roll into a ball about the size of a walnut, then put it on a plate. Repeat with the rest of the mixture until you have about 24 meatballs. Cover the plate with plastic wrap and chill in the refrigerator for an hour or overnight so the meatballs firm up (or 15 minutes in the freezer).

4 Warm a splash of olive oil in a deep skillet over medium heat. Add the meatballs. Gently fry for 5–6 minutes, until the meatballs are lightly browned. Turn them a few times so they brown evenly.

5 Lift the meatballs out of the skillet with a slotted spoon or spatula, put them on a plate, and set aside.

(continued)

6 Make the sauce. Add the onion and red bell pepper to a saucepan. Season with salt and black pepper. Keep the heat low and gently cook for 10 minutes, until the onion and pepper are soft but not colored—give them a stir every now and then.

7 Add the garlic and sumac to the saucepan. Cook and stir for 1–2 minutes, until the saucepan smells sweet and aromatic. Stir in the diced tomates and pomegranate molasses. Stir a scant 1¾ cups (200 ml) of hot water into the sauce.

8 Add the meatballs back to the saucepan and cover. Turn up the heat so the sauce starts to simmer, then turn it down again so it's just simmering gently. Cook for around 20 minutes, until the sauce has thickened a little. Stir every now and then.

9 While the meatballs and sauce simmer, cook some more quinoa to serve with the meatballs—1 cup (200 g) simmered in 2 cups (480 ml) of water for 10–15 minutes should be enough for 4 people.

10 Taste the tomato sauce and add more salt and pepper if you think it needs it. Serve the meatballs and tomato sauce with the cooked quinoa and fresh, chopped cilantro.

Sumac is a fragrant spice that is commonly used in Middle Eastern cooking. It originates from the Sumac bush and is made by drying and crushing the berries. Sumac has a lemony flavor and is commonly used as a garnish or part of the Za'atar spice mix.

QUINOA MEATBALLS VARIATION

THERE'S MORE THAN ONE WAY TO TURN A MEATBALL INTO A MEAL. FROM ROMANTIC MEATBALLS AND SPAGHETTI TO SHARE, TO A WRAP YOU CAN EAT ON THE GO, SEE WHICH STYLE SUITS YOU—OR TRY THEM ALL!

MIX UP YOUR MEATBALLS

Lamb pairs well with Middle Eastern flavors, but you can swap the ground lamb for beef, pork, or turkey if you prefer. Try using different herbs and spices too, depending on what you have at home and what you like.

SIDE SWAPS

If you want to have a different side dish, try bulgur wheat. Soak ¼ cup (40 g) per person in enough hot water to cover it, just like couscous. Leave it for 20 minutes, then drain it (if you need to) and stir in lots of freshly chopped parsley before serving it with the meatballs and tomato sauce. And, although it isn't a traditional Italian meatball and sauce mix, this recipe is also yummy with spaghetti or tagliatelle.

LAMB AND QUINOA MEATBALL WRAPS

Make the meatballs following the main recipe but instead of frying, broil them for 10–12 minutes, turning once, so they are browned and cooked through—you can thread them onto skewers to make them easier to turn. Serve them wrapped in flatbreads with chopped lettuce, cucumber, tomatoes, red onion, and fresh parsley. A spoonful of dairy-free tzatziki or plain yogurt and some ground cumin are also delicious with the wraps.

SOUPS, SALADS & SIDES

ROASTED CAULIFLOWER QUINOA SOUP

CURRY SQUASH QUINOA BISQUE WITH COCONUT CREAM

QUINOA COUSCOUS WITH BLOOD ORANGES AND BURRATA

QUINOA KISIR WITH POMEGRANATE AND WALNUTS

SUMMER QUINOA SALAD WITH GRAPEFRUIT AND TAHINI DRESSING

FRUITY QUINOA TABBOULEH WITH FETA CHEESE

BEET AND CARROT QUINOA CAKES WITH CUMIN YOGURT SAUCE

THAI-STYLE CRAB, POMELO, AND QUINOA SALAD

ROASTED WINTER VEGETABLE, QUINOA, AND WILD RICE SALAD

Recipe on page 118

ROASTED CAULIFLOWER QUINOA SOUP

SERVES	4
PREP	10 minutes
COOK	40 minutes

YOU WILL NEED

1 lb. (450 g) head of cauliflower, core cut out and chopped into florets

1 cup (160 g) diced onion

2 teaspoons olive oil

1 can (14 oz./400 g) diced tomatoes

2 cups (480 ml) vegetable stock

2½ cups (450 g) cooked white quinoa

3 cups (200 g) kale, washed, de-stemmed, and chopped

¼ cup minced fresh basil

2 tablespoons minced fresh flat-leaf parsley

salt and black pepper

(pictured on page 117)

FREE FROM
DAIRY, GLUTEN & WHEAT

IF YOU'RE LOOKING FOR A PLANT-BASED SOUP THAT IS AS FILLING AS IT IS FLAVORFUL, YOU NEED TO MAKE THIS RECIPE. ROASTED CAULIFLOWER ADDS DEPTH, THE HERBS BRING FRESHNESS, AND THE QUINOA MAKES IT SUBSTANTIAL.

1 Preheat the oven to 375°F/190°C/Gas Mark 5 and line a cookie sheet with parchment.

2 Toss the cauliflower florets and onion in the olive oil, ½ teaspoon of salt, and ¼ teaspoon of black pepper until evenly covered. Spread the mixture out in a single layer on the cookie sheet and roast for 20 minutes.

3 Once the cauliflower is roasted, transfer it to a large saucepan, warmed over medium heat. Add the tomatoes, vegetable stock, 1 cup (240 ml) of water, and quinoa to the pot and bring to a boil.

4 Reduce the heat to medium low, and add the kale, basil, and parsley to the pot. Stir and simmer for 15 minutes, covered.

5 Check the soup occasionally and add more water or vegetable stock if you feel that it is not thin enough. Season with salt and pepper and serve warm.

QUINOA SOUP VARIATIONS

A WARM SOUP LIKE THIS IS COMFORTING AND SATISFYING, BUT THERE ARE MORE WAYS TO ADAPT IT TO FIT A DIFFERENT SEASON OR INCREASE THE HEARTINESS FOR COLD NIGHTS.

(DF) (GF) (WF)

SAUSAGE OR BEANS

For an even more filling soup, add a couple of sliced links of your favorite gluten-free sausage, or a can of cannellini beans for a low-fat option.

(VG) (DF) (GF) (WF)

AUTUMNAL PUMPKIN

Give this recipe seasonal flavors by subbing pumpkin purée for the tomatoes, and using fresh thyme and sage instead of the basil and parsley.

(VG) (DF)

SOURDOUGH BOWL

This cauliflower soup would be great served in a toasted sourdough bread bowl. Just scoop out a rough sourdough loaf until the walls are 1 inch (2.5 cm) thick, brush the outside with a thin coat of garlic olive oil, and bake for 5 minutes at 375°F/190°C/Gas Mark 5, then fill with soup.

CURRY SQUASH QUINOA BISQUE WITH COCONUT CREAM

SERVES	4
PREP	15 minutes
COOK	45 minutes

YOU WILL NEED

3 lb. (1.35 kg) kabocha squash, peeled and chopped

4 garlic cloves

1 tablespoon olive oil

½ teaspoon salt

3 cups (720 ml) vegetable stock

reserved liquid from coconut milk

2 cups (380 g) cooked quinoa

2 tablespoons yellow curry powder

salt and white pepper

2 tablespoons chopped fresh chives, for serving

FOR THE COCONUT CREAM

1 can (14 fl. oz./400 ml) full-fat coconut milk, refrigerated overnight

1 teaspoon lime juice

¼ teaspoon salt

FREE FROM
DAIRY, GLUTEN & WHEAT

WHO WOULD HAVE THOUGHT THAT QUINOA COULD LEND CREAMINESS TO BISQUE WITHOUT THE UNNECESSARY FAT FROM HEAVY CREAM? THIS CURRIED BISQUE IS SUPER-COMFORTING AND SEEMS INDULGENT, TOO.

1 To make the coconut cream, separate the hardened coconut fat from the liquid and place it in a bowl. Keep the liquid for the bisque. Whisk the coconut fat with the lime juice and salt, and refrigerate until ready for serving.

2 Preheat the oven to 375°F/190°C/Gas Mark 5, and line a large cookie sheet with parchment. Toss the squash and garlic with the olive oil, salt, and ¼ teaspoon of white pepper in a large bowl. Spread the mixture on the cookie sheet and roast for 30 minutes.

3 Once the squash is roasted, put it in a blender or food processor with the vegetable stock, liquid from the coconut milk, quinoa, and curry powder. Purée until smooth—you may need to work in batches, depending on the size of your blender.

4 Transfer the blended bisque to a large pot and bring to a boil over medium heat, stirring occasionally so that the bottom does not burn. Adjust the heat to low and simmer, covered, for 10 minutes, again stirring occasionally.

5 Taste and season with more salt and white pepper if necessary. Divide the soup between four bowls and top with a large dollop of coconut cream and a few sprinkled chives. Serve immediately.

SQUASH SWAP
Can't find kabocha squash? Try using the same volume of butternut or acorn squash instead.

QUINOA COUSCOUS WITH BLOOD ORANGES AND BURRATA

SERVES	4
PREP	5 minutes
COOK	15 minutes

THIS ELEGANT QUINOA COUSCOUS SALAD IS SERVED WITH JUICY SLICES OF BLOOD ORANGE AND CREAMY BURRATA CHEESE. IT IS PERFECT FOR A LIGHT SUMMER LUNCH OR AN ALFRESCO SUPPER.

YOU WILL NEED

2 tablespoons olive oil

1 cup (200 g) uncooked quinoa

zest and juice of 1 lemon

¼ cup (30 g) pine nuts

2 tablespoons chopped fresh flat-leaf parsley, plus extra for garnish

1 tablespoon chopped fresh mint leaves, plus extra for garnish

2 blood oranges, peeled and cut into segments

9 oz. (250 g) burrata cheese

salt and black pepper

crusty bread, for serving

FREE FROM
GLUTEN & WHEAT

1 Heat the olive oil in a large saucepan that has a lid, and add the quinoa, lemon zest and juice, and pine nuts. Sauté over low heat and stir to cover all the grains with the oil and toast the nuts, before adding 1 pint (450 ml) of water along with the parsley and mint.

2 Simmer, covered, for 15 minutes, until the quinoa is cooked and has absorbed all of the liquid.

3 Season to taste with salt and black pepper and allow the dish to come to room temperature.

4 For serving, create a table centerpiece by using a single bowl or divide the quinoa between four plates and arrange the sliced blood oranges around the edge of each. Break the burrata into 4 pieces if making individual servings or leave it whole and place it in the middle of the quinoa. Garnish with extra parsley and mint, and serve with crusty bread.

COUSCOUS SALAD VARIATIONS

FROM SPICY HARISSA AND SMOKED VEGETABLES TO CRISPY PANCETTA, THESE IDEAS ARE SURE TO BE ENJOYED BY ALL THE FAMILY AS WELL AS BEING LIGHT AND HEALTHY TO EAT, TOO.

CAPRESE QUINOA COUSCOUS SALAD

In place of the burrata cheese use 9 oz. (250 g) of baby mozzarella balls. Cook the quinoa as in the main recipe on page 122 and spoon onto a large serving platter, then arrange 2 sliced plum tomatoes and the mozzarella balls over the top. Finish by scattering 1 tablespoon chopped fresh basil over the salad. Offer some extra dressing when serving: Mix the juice of 1 lemon with ⅔ cup (150 ml) extra-virgin olive oil and season to taste. Serve with sliced focaccia.

GOAT CHEESE AND ARUGULA QUINOA COUSCOUS SALAD WITH PANCETTA

Cook the quinoa as in the main recipe. Fry 1 cup (100 g) smoked pancetta cubes (or lardons) in a skillet until crisp, and set to one side. Loosely mix 4½ oz. (125 g) of arugula leaves with the cooked quinoa. Spoon the cooked quinoa and arugula onto a serving platter, or divide between four plates and then scatter the cooked pancetta over the top. Sprinkle 1 cup (150 g) crumbled goat cheese over the salad and serve with crusty bread such as a baguette.

MOROCCAN QUINOA COUSCOUS SALAD WITH ROASTED VEGETABLES AND HARISSA

Roast the following vegetables together in 2 tablespoons olive oil in a preheated oven (400°F/200°C/Gas Mark 6) for 45 minutes until cooked and slightly charred: 1 eggplant, diced small; 2 zucchini, diced small; 1 large onion, peeled and cut into quarters; 3 large tomatoes, cut into small dice. Mix the roasted vegetables with the cooked quinoa, add 1 teaspoon harissa paste, and mix well. Season to taste with salt and black pepper. Serve warm with chopped fresh flat-leaf parsley sprinkled over the top, and warm pita bread.

ARUGULA

Arugula has a wonderful peppery flavor and is easy to grow at home. Low in calories and high in antioxidants, this is truly a superfood that adds essential vitamins, minerals, taste, and texture to all kinds of recipes. Like kale, this vegetable is high in vitamin C, which boosts immunity and helps the body fight infectious diseases. Scatter a handful of arugula leaves among other salad leaves or add them to steamed seasonal greens for extra taste and flavor.

QUINOA KISIR WITH POMEGRANATE AND WALNUTS

SERVES	2
PREP	15 minutes
COOK	40 minutes

YOU WILL NEED

2 tablespoons extra-virgin olive oil

1 small onion, peeled and chopped

2 garlic cloves, peeled and minced

1 teaspoon ground cumin

1 teaspoon allspice

1 teaspoon paprika

1 red chili pepper, seeded and finely chopped

1 tablespoon tomato paste

½ cup (100 g) uncooked black quinoa

2 tomatoes, cored and diced

4 scallions, trimmed and sliced

¼ cup (50 g) pomegranate seeds

large handful of fresh flat-leaf parsley leaves and stalks, chopped

handful of fresh mint leaves, chopped

zest and juice of 1 lemon

1 tablespoon pomegranate molasses

½ cup (60 g) walnut pieces

salt and black pepper

FREE FROM DAIRY, GLUTEN & WHEAT

KISIR IS A TURKISH SALAD THAT'S SIMILAR TO TABBOULEH. FRESH FLAVORS ARE KEY—HOT CHILI, ZESTY LEMON, AND PLENTY OF FRESH HERBS. BLACK QUINOA GIVES THIS LIGHT AND ZINGY DISH A CHEWY TEXTURE AND ADDS A BIT OF DRAMA.

1 Warm 1 tablespoon of the olive oil in a saucepan. Add the onion and season with salt and black pepper. Sweat over low heat for 5–8 minutes, stirring every so often, until the onion is soft but hasn't colored. If it starts to brown, turn the heat down.

2 Stir in the garlic, cumin, allspice, paprika, chili pepper, and tomato paste. Cook and stir for 1–2 minutes, until the mixture smells aromatic.

3 Add the quinoa to the saucepan with 1 cup (240 ml) of cold water. Cover. Bring to a boil, then turn the heat down and gently simmer for 20–25 minutes, or until all the water has been absorbed and the quinoa is tender. If it looks like it's getting too dry while it cooks, add a splash more water. Drain well.

4 Transfer the cooked quinoa to a bowl. Add the tomatoes, scallions, pomegranate seeds, parsley, and mint. Stir together.

5 Add the lemon zest to the bowl. Whisk the lemon juice with the remaining 1 tablespoon of olive oil, 1 tablespoon of pomegranate molasses, and some salt and black pepper. Stir into the salad. Taste and add more salt and pepper if you think it needs it.

6 Toast the walnut pieces in a dry skillet over low heat. Shake the skillet to keep the walnut pieces moving and toast for 2–3 minutes, until they are golden brown. Stir the nuts into the kisir and serve.

COLOR CHANGE
You can make this salad with white quinoa, if you prefer. Remember, it takes less time to cook than black quinoa—around 10–15 minutes.

SUMMER QUINOA SALAD WITH GRAPEFRUIT AND TAHINI DRESSING

SERVES	4
PREP	10 minutes
COOK	35 minutes

LAYERS OF FRESH FLAVOR MAKE THIS BRIGHT CITRUSY SALAD WITH A PEPPERY BASE A SUMMERTIME STAPLE. THE DISH WORKS WITHOUT THE ASPARAGUS AS WELL, ALTHOUGH THE WARM TOPPER WORKS TO BRING OUT ITS FRAGRANT NOTES.

YOU WILL NEED

8 oz. (225 g) fresh asparagus

olive oil, for roasting

juice of ½ grapefruit (about ⅓ cup/80 ml)

1 garlic clove, minced

2 tablespoons olive oil

1 tablespoon tahini

1 tablespoon maple syrup

6 packed cups (150 g) fresh baby arugula leaves

2 cups (250 g) halved red grapes

1½ cups (270 g) cooked quinoa

½ cup (60 g) dry-roasted hazelnuts, chopped

salt and black pepper

FREE FROM
DAIRY, GLUTEN & WHEAT

1 Preheat the oven to 350°F/180°C/Gas Mark 4.

2 Arrange the asparagus on a cookie sheet, drizzle with the olive oil and sprinkle with salt. Roast in the oven for 30–35 minutes.

3 In a large bowl, whisk together the grapefruit juice, garlic, olive oil, tahini, and maple syrup. Add the arugula, grapes, quinoa, and hazelnuts, and toss with the dressing. Top with the warm asparagus, and season with salt and black pepper to taste.

FRUITY QUINOA TABBOULEH WITH FETA CHEESE

SERVES	2
PREP	15 minutes
COOK	10–15 minutes

YOU WILL NEED

¼ cup (50 g) uncooked quinoa

1 small red onion, peeled and diced

2 small tomatoes, cored and diced

very large handful of fresh flat-leaf parsley leaves and stalks, finely chopped

large handful of fresh mint leaves, finely chopped

⅛ cup (20 g) chopped dried apricots

½ cup (70 g) dried cranberries

⅛ cup (15 g) chopped pistachios

zest and juice of 1 lemon

1 teaspoon allspice

2 tablespoons extra-virgin olive oil

generous ⅔ cup (115 g) crumbled feta cheese

salt and black pepper

FREE FROM
GLUTEN & WHEAT

GREEN WITH PARSLEY AND MINT, AND FLAVORED WITH VIBRANT LEMON AND WARMING ALLSPICE, TABBOULEH MAKES A GREAT LIGHT MEAL—OR HAVE IT AS PART OF A MEZZE PLATTER FOR A MIDDLE EASTERN FEAST.

1 Put the quinoa in a saucepan with ½ cup (120 ml) of cold water. Cover. Bring to a boil, then turn the heat down and gently simmer for 10–15 minutes, or until all the water has been absorbed and the quinoa is tender. If it looks like it's getting too dry while it cooks, add a splash more water. Drain well.

2 Transfer the cooked quinoa to a bowl. Add the red onion, tomatoes, parsley, mint, apricots, cranberries, and pistachios. Stir it all together until well combined.

3 Add the lemon zest to the tabbouleh with the allspice.

4 Whisk the lemon juice with the olive oil and some salt and black pepper, then stir into the tabbouleh. Taste and add more salt and pepper if you think it needs it.

5 Top the tabbouleh with the crumbled feta cheese for serving.

MEZZE PLANS: Combine with recipes on pages 68, 112, and 126 to build up a Levantine feast. Serve with some falafel and hummus.

RINSE FIRST

Feta is a brined cheese and normally comes sealed in a little pouch with some brine to keep it from drying out. Give it a gentle rinse under cold water and pat dry with paper towels to reduce the salty flavor.

QUINOA TABBOULEH VARIATIONS
TABBOULEH IS AN EASY SALAD TO ADAPT TO WHAT'S IN SEASON OR IN YOUR REFRIGERATOR. A MIX OF HERBS, GRAINS, GREENS, AND SPICES IS ALL YOU NEED.

WINTER GREENS QUINOA TABBOULEH
Follow the main recipe on page 130 but swap the parsley and mint for blanched and shredded winter greens such as kale or cabbage, and use chopped walnuts instead of pistachios. To blanch the greens, bring a saucepan of water to a boil. Discard any thick stalks and finely shred the leaves, then add them to the saucepan of boiling water. Simmer for 2 minutes. Drain and rinse under cold water. Shake off any excess water and mix into the tabbouleh with the rest of the ingredients.

SICILIAN QUINOA TABBOULEH
Swap the mint for fresh basil and the cranberries for raisins per the main recipe. Use 1 teaspoon red pepper flakes instead of the allspice and add toasted pine nuts instead of the pistachios along with ¼ cup (50 g) pitted green olives. Omit the feta cheese. Warm a dry skillet, then put in the pine nuts. Toast for 2 minutes until the nuts are golden. They will toast very quickly and burn easily, so keep shaking the skillet and don't take your eyes off the pine nuts while they're cooking.

FETA AND WATERMELON QUINOA TABBOULEH
Omit the dried apricots and cranberries per the main recipe. Instead, stir in 2 cups (310 g) peeled and chopped watermelon with 1 teaspoon ground cumin instead of the allspice.

FETA CHEESE

Greek feta—and only feta made in Greece can be called feta—is a tangy cheese that is made with sheep's milk and is a salad's best friend. Greek salad can't be made without it, but feta's crumbly texture and salty flavor also pairs well with fresh, crunchy vegetables. Try crumbling it over honey-roasted carrots, slices of sweet melon (especially watermelon), slices of juicy cucumber and tomatoes, ribbons of zucchini, charred chunks of eggplant, into potato salads and coleslaws, or with wilted winter greens. It also cooks nicely in the oven. Sprinkle it on top of stuffed vegetables and bake until golden or wrap it in aluminum foil with fresh herbs, ground black pepper, lemon zest, and a little olive oil and bake for 10–15 minutes at 350°F/180°C/Gas Mark 4 until soft. Serve with crudites for dipping.

BEET AND CARROT QUINOA CAKES WITH CUMIN YOGURT SAUCE

THESE LITTLE CAKES ARE A HIT WITH FAMILY MEMBERS LARGE AND SMALL. PACKED WITH EARTHY, SWEET ROOT VEGETABLES, THEY'RE A GREAT EXAMPLE OF HOW QUINOA DOESN'T NEED THE STARRING ROLE TO MAKE A BIG CONTRIBUTION TO A MEAL.

MAKES	18 cakes
PREP	20 minutes
COOK	30 minutes

YOU WILL NEED

1 tablespoon cumin seeds

1 cup (180 g) cooked quinoa

1 beet, peeled and shredded

2 carrots, peeled and shredded

1 shallot, minced

¼ cup (15 g) chopped fresh cilantro

1 teaspoon fine sea salt

2 eggs

½ cup (60 g) all-purpose flour

1 teaspoon baking powder

1 tablespoon olive oil, for frying

black pepper

FOR THE SAUCE

½ cup (140 g) plain Greek-style yogurt

zest of 1 lime

1 tablespoon fresh lime juice

1 garlic clove, minced

½ teaspoon fine sea salt

½ teaspoon ground cumin

2 tablespoons chopped fresh cilantro

pinch of ground cayenne pepper (optional)

black pepper

1 To make the sauce, combine all the ingredients in a small bowl and set it aside to rest while you make the quinoa cakes.

2 Place the cumin seeds in a skillet over medium-high heat. Toast for about 2 minutes, shaking the skillet a few times, until very fragrant and lightly browned. Pour the seeds into a large mixing bowl.

3 Add the quinoa, beet, carrot, shallot, cilantro, salt, and a few grinds of black pepper. Mix well. Clear some space on one side of the bowl and crack the eggs in. Beat thoroughly, then incorporate the eggs into the vegetable mixture. Sprinkle the flour and baking powder over the mixture then stir to incorporate.

4 Heat the olive oil over medium-high heat until shimmering. Spoon about ¼ cup (60 ml) of batter into the skillet for each cake, gently spreading to form cakes about ¼ inch (6 mm) thick. Cook 4 or 5 cakes at a time so you don't crowd the skillet. Cook for 4 minutes on the first side, then flip and cook for 3–4 minutes on the second side. You may need to adjust the heat so that the cakes brown nicely on the outside while cooking thoroughly on the inside.

5 Set the cooked cakes on a wire rack or paper towel-lined plate. Add a little more oil to the skillet and continue cooking in batches until you've used all the batter. Serve warm or at room temperature with the cumin yogurt sauce.

THAI-STYLE CRAB, POMELO, AND QUINOA SALAD

SERVES	2
PREP	20 minutes
COOK	15–20 minutes

CITRUS AND SEAFOOD ALWAYS MAKE A GOOD MIX. INSPIRED BY HOT, SHARP, SWEET THAI SALADS, HERE JUICY POMELO IS PAIRED WITH DELICATE WHITE CRAB AND PLENTY OF CILANTRO.

YOU WILL NEED

¼ cup (50 g) uncooked red quinoa

½ pomelo, peeled and the flesh picked from the membrane

4 shallots, peeled and finely sliced

large handful fresh cilantro leaves

¼ cup (40 g) raw peanuts

⅓ cup (150 g) white crabmeat

1 mild red chili pepper, sliced

juice of 1 lime

1 tablespoon fish sauce

1½ tablespoons light soft brown sugar

salt

FREE FROM
DAIRY, GLUTEN & WHEAT

1 Put the quinoa in a saucepan with ½ cup (120 ml) of cold water. Cover. Bring to a boil, then turn the heat right down and gently simmer for 15–20 minutes, or until all the water has been absorbed and the quinoa is tender. If it looks like it's getting too dry while it cooks, add a splash more water. Drain well.

2 Transfer the cooked quinoa to a bowl. Add the pomelo, shallots, and cilantro leaves and mix together.

3 Warm a dry skillet over medium heat. Put in the peanuts and cook, stirring, for 3–4 minutes until the nuts are golden brown and smell toasted. Turn them out of the skillet, let them cool for a few minutes, then roughly chop them.

4 Arrange the quinoa on a couple of plates or one big serving plate. Top with the peanuts, crabmeat, and sliced chili pepper.

5 Whisk the lime juice with the fish sauce and sugar. Taste and add a pinch of salt if it's needed. Drizzle over the salad for serving.

CAN'T FIND POMELO?
Pomelos are huge citrus fruits with sweetish flesh that you can easily pick out from the thin membranes. You can swap in a grapefruit if you can't get hold of one. Just slice off the skin and then use a sharp knife to slice the flesh out of the thin membranes around each segment. Add the grapefruit flesh to the salad just like the pomelo.

ROASTED WINTER VEGETABLE, QUINOA, AND WILD RICE SALAD

SERVES	4–8
PREP	20 minutes
COOK	45 minutes

YOU WILL NEED

2½ cups (600 ml) good vegetable stock

1 teaspoon dried herbes de Provence

1 garlic clove, smashed

1 teaspoon fine sea salt

½ cup (80 g) wild rice

½ cup (100 g) uncooked red quinoa

3 carrots, trimmed, peeled, and cut into ¾-in. (2 cm) pieces

2 purple or golden beets, trimmed, peeled, and cut into ¾-in. (2 cm) pieces

3 parsnips, trimmed, peeled, and cut into ¾-in. (2 cm) pieces

1 tablespoon olive oil

⅓ cup (20 g) chopped fresh flat-leaf parsley

FREE FROM
DAIRY, GLUTEN & WHEAT

THIS HEARTY SALAD WORKS EQUALLY WELL AS A MAIN COURSE OR AS AN ACCOMPANIMENT TO OTHER DISHES. THE HINT OF ORANGE IN THE DRESSING BRINGS ALL OF THE FLAVORS TOGETHER BEAUTIFULLY.

1 Preheat the oven to 400°F/200°C/Gas Mark 6.

2 In a covered medium pot, bring the stock to a boil with the herbes de Provence, garlic, and ½ teaspoon of the salt (if the stock is unsalted). When it boils, add the wild rice, cover, reduce to a simmer, and cook for 30 minutes. Stir in the quinoa and simmer for 15 minutes more. Remove from the heat and let sit for 10 minutes before uncovering and fluffing with a fork.

3 Meanwhile, toss the root vegetables with the olive oil and the remaining salt on a rimmed cookie sheet big enough to accommodate them in a single layer without crowding. Roast in the center of the oven, turning once or twice with a spatula, until browned on the outside and tender throughout, about 30 minutes.

4 To make the dressing, place the shallot in a small bowl, pour in the sherry vinegar and orange juice, and let sit for 15 minutes. Then add the orange zest, honey, mustard, salt, and pepper, and whisk to combine. Whisk in the olive oil.

5 Combine the rice and quinoa with the roasted vegetables in a large mixing bowl. While still warm, pour the dressing over the salad and toss gently. Stir in the parsley. Serve warm or at room temperature.

BAKES & DESSERTS

FLUFFY AND FRUITY QUINOA SCONES

POWER BOOST SNICKERDOODLES

CHOCOLATE PEANUT BUTTER CANDY BARS

RICH AND FUDGY QUINOA BROWNIES

QUINOA CINNAMON POWER BITES

BLUEBERRY PISTACHIO QUINOA PARFAIT WITH QUINOA PRALINE

SPICED CASHEW "CHEESECAKE" WITH RED QUINOA CRUST

FROSTED ORANGE, SEMOLINA, AND QUINOA LAYER CAKE

APPLE CRISP WITH QUINOA CRUMBLE TOPPING

MULTISEED AND QUINOA BREAD

Recipe on page 152

FLUFFY AND FRUITY QUINOA SCONES

MAKES	12
PREP	5 minutes
COOK	10–15 minutes

YOU WILL NEED

1 ½ cups (180 g) quinoa flour, plus more for rolling

⅔ cup (80 g) coconut flour

⅔ cup (80 g) cornmeal

½ teaspoon sea salt

1 ½ teaspoons baking powder

½ teaspoon baking soda

¼ cup (50 g) sugar

6 tablespoons (85 g) unsalted butter

generous 1 cup (150 g) mixed dried fruit

zest of 1 large orange

½ cup (120 ml) buttermilk

butter and preserves, for serving

FREE FROM
GLUTEN & WHEAT

SERVE THESE FRUITY QUINOA SCONES WARM FROM THE OVEN WITH BUTTER, AND MAYBE SOME HONEY AND JAM FOR A SPECIAL WEEKEND BRUNCH. THEY ALSO MAKE A GREAT SNACK.

1 Preheat the oven to 425°F/220°C/Gas Mark 7, and line a large cookie sheet with parchment.

2 Put all of the flours, the salt, baking powder, baking soda, and sugar in a mixing bowl, and rub in the butter with your fingers until the mixture resembles fine breadcrumbs.

3 Add the dried fruit and orange zest and mix well.

4 Make a well in the center and pour in the buttermilk, then mix to incorporate all of the ingredients until you have a ball of dough. Don't overwork the dough or the scones will be tough.

5 Put the dough on a floured board and roll out to about 1-inch (2.5 cm) thickness. Stamp out 12 scones with a 2-inch (5-cm) cutter, then put them on the cookie sheet.

6 Bake for 10–15 minutes, until well risen and golden brown.

7 Serve warm with butter and preserves.

QUINOA SCONE VARIATIONS
SWEET AND SAVORY SCONES WILL EASILY FIT IN TO ANY SCHOOL OR OFFICE LUNCHBOX AND ARE A CUTE CHOICE FOR PICNICS, TOO. THESE ADDITIONAL IDEAS TICK ALL THE TASTE AND CONVENIENCE BOXES FOR ALL OCCASIONS.

CRANBERRY AND BLUEBERRY WHOLE-WHEAT SCONES
Follow the main recipe on page 142 but use 1¹/₃ cups (160 g) whole-wheat flour in place of the coconut flour and cornmeal, and replace the mixed dried fruit with 1 cup (140 g) dried cranberries and blueberries. Serve warm, split, and spread with butter for an afternoon treat.

MEXICAN CHEESE AND JALAPEÑO SAVORY SCONES
Simply omit the coconut flour, sugar, dried fruit, and orange zest in the main recipe, and in their place add an extra ²/₃ cup (80 g) cornmeal; 1½ cups (150 g) shredded cheddar cheese; 3 tablespoons canned jalapeño peppers, drained and finely chopped; and 1 teaspoon dried oregano. Make as in the main recipe, and bake for 10–15 minutes. Serve warm with butter, tomato salsa, and salad, or with chili, stews, or soups.

PLAIN BUTTERMILK BISCUITS
If you want a plain, light, and crumbly biscuit, these are just right. Follow the main recipe but replace the coconut flour and cornmeal with 1¹/₃ cups (160 g) all-purpose white flour. Omit the sugar, dried fruit, and orange zest and add an extra ½ teaspoon of baking powder to the dry ingredients before rubbing in the butter and following the method on page 142. Serve alongside a cooked breakfast or use in a breakfast sandwich. These are also excellent when used as a sweet or savory cobbler topping.

CRANBERRIES
Cranberries are billed as one of the world's healthiest foods. Acting as a strong barrier to bacteria, these ruby-red fruits pack a punch when it comes to the list of vitamins they contain—they are high in vitamins C, E, and K, and are also a very good source of antioxidants and minerals. Dried cranberries can be scattered over cereal and porridge as well as being added to bakes, cakes, and salads—there's no need to wait until Christmas to enjoy them.

POWER BOOST SNICKERDOODLES

MAKES	24
PREP	15 minutes, plus chilling
COOK	15 minutes

YOU WILL NEED

2 tablespoons freshly ground flaxseed

½ cup (120 g) nondairy butter

1 cup (200 g) sugar

½ cup (90 g) cooked quinoa

1 ½ cups (180 g) gluten-free all-purpose flour

1 ½ teaspoons cream of tartar

1 teaspoon baking powder

½ teaspoon salt

1 ½ tablespoons ground cinnamon, for rolling

FREE FROM
DAIRY, GLUTEN & WHEAT

QUINOA ADDS A PROTEIN BOOST TO EVERYONE'S FAVORITE CLASSIC COOKIE.

1 Combine the flaxseed with ⅓ cup (80 ml) of warm water, and set aside (this creates a binding gel).

2 In a large mixing bowl, cream together the butter and ¾ cup of sugar. Add the quinoa, but do not stir together. Add the flour, and do not stir. Add the cream of tartar, baking powder, and salt on top of the flour, and stir into the flour before stirring everything together. The dough should come together in a ball. Put the bowl of dough in the refrigerator to chill for about I hour.

3 Preheat the oven to 350°F/180°C/Gas Mark 4, and line a cookie sheet with parchment.

4 Combine the remaining ¼ cup of sugar with the ground cinnamon. When the dough has cooled, remove it from the refrigerator. Using your hands, roll the pieces of dough into I-inch (2.5 cm) balls, roll them through the cinnamon sugar, and place them on the cookie sheet. Use all the dough, and place the balls 2 inches (5 cm) apart on cookie sheet.

5 Bake for 13–15 minutes.

6 Cool completely before storing in an airtight container. The cookies will keep for up to I week at room temperature or for 2 weeks in the refrigerator.

CHOCOLATE PEANUT BUTTER CANDY BARS

MAKES	20–22
PREP	12 minutes, plus setting
COOK	5 minutes

YOU WILL NEED

1 cup (180 g) pitted dried dates

¾ cup (90 g) raw cashew nuts

⅓ cup (80 g) peanut butter

⅓ cup (60 g) cooked quinoa

¼ cup (25 g) almond meal

3½ oz. (100 g) organic dark chocolate (70% cocoa solids), chopped

FREE FROM
DAIRY, GLUTEN
& WHEAT

THESE CHOCOLATE-COVERED BARS ARE PACKED WITH PROTEIN AND FLAVOR—AND YOU CAN ENJOY THEM ANY TIME! THIS DOUGH CAN ALSO BE FORMED INTO BALLS AND ROLLED THROUGH MELTED CHOCOLATE TO MAKE ELEGANT TRUFFLES.

1 Line a cookie sheet with parchment.

2 Put the dates in a food processor or blender, and pulse until crumbly. Remove the dates, then add the cashews to the food processor or blender and pulse to a crumble. Combine the dates and cashews in a mixing bowl. Alternatively, chop the dates and cashews to a coarse crumb and combine.

3 Add the peanut butter, cooked quinoa, and almond meal to the date and cashew mixture. Stir to combine.

4 Using your hands, form the dough into a rectangle shape on the cookie sheet, then use a rolling pin to smooth it into an even layer. Transfer to the refrigerator for about 4 hours, until set.

5 Once set, cut into individual bar shapes. Melt the chocolate in a small heatproof bowl set over a saucepan of gently simmering water. Once melted, dip one side of each bar into the chocolate, and return to the cookie sheet to set.

6 Serve immediately or store the bars in an airtight container in the refrigerator for 7–10 days.

CANDY BAR VARIATIONS

SWAP INGREDIENTS TO CREATE A RANGE OF DIFFERENT PROTEIN-PACKED BARS. MILD SUNFLOWER SEED BUTTER LETS SWEET BANANA CHIPS SHINE, WHILE ADDING WALNUTS PROVIDES POWERFUL NUTRIENTS THAT ARE SAID TO PROMOTE HEART AND BRAIN HEALTH.

VANILLA APRICOT BARS

Follow the main recipe on page 148, but replace the peanut butter with ⅓ cup (80 g) sunflower seed butter, replace the dates with 1 cup (160 g) chopped dried apricots, and replace the almond meal with ¼ cup (25 g) vanilla protein powder.

BANANA CRUNCH BARS

Follow the main recipe, but replace ¼ cup (30 g) of the cashews with banana chips, and replace the peanut butter with sunflower seed butter.

COCONUT WALNUT BARS

Follow the main recipe, but replace the cashew nuts with walnuts, add ¼ cup (18 g) shredded coconut and ½ teaspoon of salt, and combine with the dates.

NUT BUTTERS

The popularity of nut butters has exploded in recent years—people love the fact that they are so easy to make at home! Packed with heart healthy "good" fats, essential proteins, vitamins, and minerals, nut butters are a delicious way to get your daily nutrients. The recipe ideas are endless—keep it savory by stirring a nut butter into a spicy soup or a Thai-inspired noodle dish. Sweets like cookies, energy bars, and truffles always welcome a nut butter infusion. And this combination of nut butter and chocolate? A classic!

RICH AND FUDGY QUINOA BROWNIES

MAKES	16
PREP	10 minutes
COOK	45 minutes, plus cooling

YOU WILL NEED

butter or nonstick cooking spray, for greasing

6 oz. (175 g) bittersweet chocolate (60% cocoa solids), chopped

8 tablespoons butter, diced

¾ cup (150 g) sugar

¾ cup (130 g) light brown sugar

3 eggs

1 cup (190 g) cooked quinoa

1 tablespoon vanilla extract

½ teaspoon fine sea salt

3 tablespoons organic cornstarch

¼ cup (30 g) cocoa powder

1 cup (120 g) chopped walnuts or pecans (optional)

FREE FROM
GLUTEN & WHEAT

THESE BROWNIES ARE INDULGENT, WITH THAT COVETED SHINY, CRACKLY LAYER ON TOP. YOU'D NEVER GUESS THAT THEY CONTAIN QUINOA AND ARE GLUTEN-FREE.

1 Preheat the oven to 350°F/180°C/Gas Mark 4 with a rack in the center. Line the bottom and sides of an 8-inch (20-cm) square baking pan with aluminum foil, and butter the foil or spray.

2 Put the chocolate and the butter in a large microwave-safe bowl. Heat at medium power for about 90 seconds and then in 30-second bursts if necessary, stirring well between heatings to incorporate any unmelted bits. Alternatively, melt the chocolate and butter together in the top of a double boiler, stirring frequently.

3 Add the white and brown sugars. Stir vigorously with a silicone spatula or wooden spoon until the sugar is well incorporated.

4 Put the eggs, quinoa, vanilla, and salt in a blender. Sift in the cornstarch and cocoa powder. Blend the mixture until it's completely smooth, about 1 minute.

5 Pour the egg mixture into the bowl with the chocolate mixture. Stir vigorously for 2–3 minutes, until the batter is shiny and smooth. Mix in the chopped nuts, if using.

6 Pour the batter into the prepared baking pan. Gently tap it on the counter a few times to remove any air bubbles. Bake for 45 minutes.

7 Let cool for 10 minutes on a rack, then gently lift the brownies out of the pan using the foil, and let cool completely in the foil on a rack. Don't rush the cooling process, or the brownies will be difficult to cut. Gently peel the foil off the brownies and, using a long, thin knife dipped in hot water and wiped with a paper towel between cuts, cut into 16 (2 inch/5 cm) squares.

EASY LINER
A great way to line the baking pan with foil is to turn the pan upside down, cut a square of foil from the roll, and mold the foil to the outside of the pan. Then just turn the pan right side up and press the foil into the pan.

QUINOA CINNAMON POWER BITES

MAKES	20
PREP	8 minutes
COOK	20 minutes

YOU WILL NEED

1 can (14 oz./400 g) chickpeas, drained and rinsed

½ cup (90 g) cooked quinoa

⅓ cup (67 g) sugar

¼ cup (25 g) almond flour

⅓ cup (80 g) almond butter

1 tablespoon ground cinnamon

½ tablespoon cardamom

FREE FROM
DAIRY, GLUTEN
& WHEAT

THIS MAKE-AHEAD RECIPE IS A PERFECT ON-THE-GO BREAKFAST BITE OR GO-TO WORKOUT SNACK. GROUP THE BITES IN BAGS OF THREE, AND ENJOY WITH A BREAKFAST SMOOTHIE OR AS AN AFTERNOON PICK-ME-UP.

1 In a food processor, pulse the chickpeas until crumbly, about 1 minute. Add the cooked quinoa, sugar, and almond flour and pulse to combine, about 30 seconds. Scrape down the sides of the bowl with a spatula. Add the almond butter, cinnamon, and cardamom, and process until a dough ball forms.

2 Transfer the dough ball to a clean bowl and put it in the refrigerator.

3 Heat the oven to 350°F/180°C/Gas Mark 4, and line a cookie sheet with parchment. Once the oven has reached the correct temperature, remove the dough from the refrigerator. Using a tablespoon, spoon golf-ball-size scoops and, using your hands, roll them into balls. Place them on the cookie sheet and continue with the rest of dough.

4 Bake for 20 minutes, or until the cookies are cooked through.

NO-BAKE BITES
These snacks can also be made without baking. Simply place the balls on the cookie sheet in the refrigerator to set. Transfer to an airtight container and store in the refrigerator.

POWER BITE VARIATIONS

TRY ADDING THE BRIGHT, TART FLAVOR OF CITRUS FRUIT OR DRIED CHERRIES TO YOUR POWER BITES—OR MIX IN CHOCOLATE AND WALNUTS FOR ADDED DEPTH.

CHOCOLATE CRUNCH POWER BITES

To the chickpeas, cooked quinoa, sugar, almond butter, and almond flour, add ½ cup (75 g) vegan chocolate chips and ⅓ cup (40 g) chopped walnuts. Leave out the cinnamon and cardamon.

TART CHERRY POWER BITES

To the chickpeas, cooked quinoa, sugar, and almond flour, add ⅓ cup (80 g) sunflower seed butter in place of the almond butter, ½ cup (70 g) dried cherries, and the zest of 1 lemon. Omit the cinnamon and cardamon.

SUMMER CITRUS POWER BITES

To the chickpeas, cooked quinoa, sugar, and almond flour, add ⅓ cup (80 g) sunflower seed butter, 2–3 drops pure orange extract, and the zest of 2 lemons.

CINNAMON

Cinnamon is a spice that has long been renowned for its medicinal properties, from heart health to blood sugar regulation. To gain the benefits of cinnamon, add it to more of your foods: Stir it into your chili for a hint of spice, sprinkle it into your coffee for a warming spike, top your morning oatmeal, or dust over a slice of peanut butter toast. For something lighter, you could add it to a bowl of fresh fruit, or swirl it into a serving of creamy yogurt.

BLUEBERRY PISTACHIO QUINOA PARFAIT WITH QUINOA PRALINE

SERVES	4
PREP	5 minutes, plus cooling
COOK	30 minutes

THIS FANCY DESSERT IS AS DELECTABLE AS IT IS GORGEOUS. BRIGHT, CREAMY QUINOA PROVIDES AN EXCELLENT CANVAS FOR FRESH BLUEBERRIES AND GREEN PISTACHIOS. THE GAME-CHANGER HERE, THOUGH, IS THE BEAUTIFUL TRICOLOR QUINOA PRALINE.

FOR THE CREAMY QUINOA

1 cup (200 g) uncooked tricolor quinoa

2½ cups (600 ml) nondairy milk

6 tablespoons maple syrup

1 teaspoon vanilla extract

¼ cup (60 g) chia seeds

FOR THE QUINOA PRALINE

⅓ cup (60 g) uncooked tricolor quinoa

3 tablespoons sugar

3 tablespoons light brown sugar

¾ teaspoon vanilla extract

1½ tablespoons coconut oil

1½ tablespoons nondairy milk

pinch of salt

FOR THE FILLINGS

1 cup (150 g) fresh blueberries

½ cup (60 g) roasted salted pistachios

FREE FROM
DAIRY, GLUTEN & WHEAT

1 To make the creamy quinoa, put all of the ingredients, except for the chia seeds, in a large saucepan. Cover partially with a lid and simmer over medium-low heat for 20 minutes, or until the quinoa is soft. There will be excess liquid.

2 Stir the chia seeds into the creamy quinoa, transfer to a bowl, and refrigerate for 1 hour, or until chilled.

3 To make the praline, while the creamy quinoa is cooling, warm a skillet over medium heat. Once hot, add the quinoa to the skillet and move the seeds around occasionally so that they do not burn.

4 Once the quinoa starts to pop, cover the saucepan with a lid and continue to keep the seeds moving for 5–10 minutes. Lower the heat if the quinoa starts to smoke heavily. Popping quinoa should have a similar aroma to popping corn.

(continued)

5 When the quinoa has darkened slightly and smells toasted, set the skillet aside. Place the toasted quinoa and the rest of the praline ingredients in a saucepan and warm, covered, over medium heat.

6 Line a cookie sheet with parchment or a silicone mat. Bring the praline mixture to a boil, stirring often, and making sure none of the sugar crystals are missed. Cook until all sugar is dissolved and test the texture by dropping a tiny amount into a glass of cold water; when picked out, it should be soft and flexible.

7 Take the saucepan off the stove and stir vigorously until the praline pulls away from the sides of the saucepan. Place 8 spoonfuls onto the cookie sheet and cool for 10 minutes.

8 Have ready four short, wide glasses. Make a parfait by spooning 5 tablespoons of creamy quinoa into a glass, then 2 tablespoons of blueberries, 1 tablespoon of pistachios, and one round of crumbled praline, then repeat for a second round of everything and top with intact praline instead of crumbled. Do this for all the glasses and serve chilled.

QUINOA PARFAIT VARIATIONS

AS PERFECT AS THIS BEAUTIFUL BLUEBERRY PISTACHIO DESSERT IS, THERE ARE CERTAINLY WAYS TO TRY OUT AN ASSORTMENT OF PREPARATIONS AND FLAVORS WHILE KEEPING IT CLASSY.

APPLE AND CASHEW

If you don't like blueberries or pistachios, try using diced Fuji or Gala apples and roasted cashews instead. Add ½ teaspoon ground cinnamon to the creamy quinoa to pair with the apples for this variation.

PARTY PARFAIT

You can easily make this recipe great for parties by preparing it in a large trifle dish instead of the separate glasses.

MINT CHOCOLATE

Make a mint chocolate version of this parfait by adding ¼ teaspoon of mint extract to the creamy quinoa after it is done cooking and using I cup (150 g) chopped dark chocolate (70 percent cocoa solids) as a filling ingredient in place of the blueberries.

SPICED CASHEW "CHEESECAKE" WITH RED QUINOA CRUST

RED QUINOA MAKES A GREAT SUBSTITUTE FOR GRAHAM CRACKERS OR FLOUR IN THIS CHEESECAKE CRUST. THE QUINOA FLOUR GIVES IT A GREAT CRUNCH AND A DISTINCT FLAVOR THAT PAIRS PERFECTLY WITH THE CREAMY, SWEET CHEESECAKE FILLING.

SERVES	6
PREP	5 minutes, plus soaking and cooling
COOK	30 minutes

YOU WILL NEED

2 cups (240 g) raw cashews

¼ cup (60 ml) melted unrefined coconut oil, plus extra for greasing

3 tablespoons maple syrup

2 tablespoons lemon juice

2 tablespoons water

2 teaspoons ground cinnamon

1½ teaspoons vanilla extract

FOR THE CRUST

½ cup (100 g) uncooked red quinoa

3 tablespoons unrefined coconut oil

3 tablespoons coconut sugar

1 teaspoon minced fresh ginger root

pinch of ground nutmeg

pinch of salt

FREE FROM
DAIRY, GLUTEN & WHEAT

1 Preheat the oven to 350°F/180°C/Gas Mark 4, and lightly grease a 6-inch (15-cm) springform pan with coconut oil.

2 Start by making the crust. Rinse and dry the red quinoa, then put it in a food processor and pulse until it has a sand-like texture, similar to almond meal.

3 Add the coconut oil, coconut sugar, ginger, nutmeg, and salt to the processor and pulse until evenly combined. Firmly press the crust mixture into the bottom of the springform pan.

4 Bake for 5 minutes, then set the pan on a cooling rack until fully cooled. Wait until fully cooled and then place in the refrigerator to firm up.

5 While the crust is cooling, soak the cashews in a bowl of hot water for 20–30 minutes, or until soft. Drain and rinse.

6 Put the cashews and the filling ingredients into a high-speed blender and purée until very smooth. Pour the filling into the springform pan and tap it down on a stable surface to spread it evenly and remove major air bubbles.

7 Bake the cheesecake for 20–25 minutes, or until the edges have browned and pulled away from the sides of the pan slightly. The cheesecake will not jiggle much. Let the cheesecake cool on a cooling rack, then refrigerate for at least 4–6 hours. Served chilled.

PRESS IT DOWN
Use a flat-bottomed
measuring cup or
glass to help press the
crust evenly into the
springform pan.

FROSTED ORANGE, SEMOLINA, AND QUINOA LAYER CAKE

SERVES	12
PREP	5 minutes
COOK	30 minutes

YOU WILL NEED

butter or nonstick cooking spray, for greasing

1 cup (180 g) cooked quinoa

1 cup (180 g) cooked semolina

4 eggs

zest and juice of 2 oranges

¾ cup (180 ml) coconut oil

2 teaspoons baking powder

½ teaspoon salt

FOR THE FROSTING

1 can (14 fl. oz./400 ml) full-fat coconut milk, refrigerated overnight

¾ cup (100 g) confectioners' sugar

zest of 1 orange, plus extra for topping

FREE FROM
DAIRY, GLUTEN
& WHEAT

THIS BEAUTIFUL CAKE IS DAIRY-FREE, AS IT USES COCONUT OIL IN THE SPONGE AS WELL AS FOR THE FROSTING! IT'S A FABULOUS SHOW-STOPPING CAKE FOR ANY SPECIAL OCCASION.

1 Preheat the oven to 350°F/180°C/Gas Mark 4. Use the butter or spray to grease two 8-inch (20-cm) cake pans, and then line with parchment.

2 Put the quinoa, semolina, eggs, zest and juice, coconut oil, baking powder, and salt in a large mixing bowl and beat with hand mixer for 2 minutes. Adjust the thickness if too liquid with a little more quinoa or semolina—the consistency should be like a very thick batter.

3 Divide the cake mixture between the two pans and bake for 30 minutes, until risen and golden brown.

4 Let the cake cool in the pans for 2 minutes, then turn out onto a wire rack to cool completely.

5 To make the frosting: Whip the coconut milk with the confectioners' sugar and orange zest until light and fluffy. Put the frosting in the refrigerator to thicken.

6 To decorate the cake, spread half of the frosting over one cake and add the other layer on top, positioning it so the edges align. Swirl the remaining frosting over the top and sides of the cake, and decorate with a little extra orange zest. Or leave the sides free from frosting so you can see the layers and spread all of the frosting on the top, as shown in the picture.

7 Slice the cake and serve.

APPLE CRISP WITH QUINOA CRUMBLE TOPPING

SERVES	8
PREP	20 minutes
COOK	1 hour 20 minutes

YOU WILL NEED

3 lb. (1.3 kg) apples

1 tablespoon lemon juice

⅓ cup (65 g) sugar

3 tablespoons all-purpose flour

1 teaspoon ground cinnamon

¼ teaspoon ground nutmeg

⅛ teaspoon fine sea salt

FOR THE TOPPING

½ cup (100 g) uncooked quinoa

¾ cup (75 g) rolled oats

¾ cup (130 g) light brown sugar

¾ cup (90 g) all-purpose flour

8 tablespoons butter, diced

vanilla cream, for serving

TRY A MIX OF GRANNY SMITH APPLES AND A SWEETER BAKING APPLE SUCH AS PINK LADY OR HONEYCRISP FOR THIS DESSERT. ANY APPLE PIE VARIETY WILL WORK WELL.

1 Preheat the oven to 375°F/190°C/Gas Mark 5 with a rack in the center. While the oven heats, spread the quinoa on a rimmed cookie sheet and dry in the oven for 10 minutes. Pour into a small mixing bowl and set aside to cool.

2 To make the filling, peel, core, and slice the apples into ¼-inch (6-mm) thick slices. Put them in a large mixing bowl and toss with the lemon juice. Sprinkle the sugar, flour, cinnamon, nutmeg, and salt onto the apples and toss gently until the apples are evenly coated.

3 To make the topping, to the bowl with the quinoa, add and toss together the oats, brown sugar, and flour. Add the diced butter and use your fingers to pinch the butter into the quinoa mixture until it forms a coarse crumble with no loose bits of dry ingredients.

4 Place a deep-dish pie pan or a 2-quart oven-safe dish onto a cookie sheet to catch any drips. Pour the apple mixture into the dish and sprinkle evenly with the crumble topping.

5 Bake until the filling is soft and bubbly and the topping is nicely browned, 65–75 minutes, covering loosely with aluminum foil when the topping is sufficiently browned (around the 45-minute mark). Let cool for 10 minutes or so, and serve warm with vanilla cream.

EASY GLUTEN-FREE
For a gluten-free version, use gluten-free oats, substitute the flour in the topping with gluten-free flour, and replace the flour in the filling with 2 tablespoons of cornstarch.

FRUIT CRISP VARIATIONS

AT HEART, A CRISP IS A FLEXIBLE DESSERT THAT HIGHLIGHTS SEASONAL FRUIT AND HELPS YOU DEAL WITH BUMPER CROPS. HERE ARE A COUPLE OF WAYS TO INCORPORATE SPRING AND SUMMER PRODUCE INTO THIS RECIPE.

BLUEBERRY CRISP

For the filling, replace the apples with 7½ cups (1.3 kg) fresh or frozen blueberries. Reduce the sugar to ¼ cup (50 g) and swap in 2 tablespoons of cornstarch for the flour. Omit the cinnamon and nutmeg.

STRAWBERRY RHUBARB CRISP

For the filling, replace the apples with 3 cups (450 g) chopped fresh rhubarb stalks and 3 cups (450 g) hulled, halved strawberries. Increase the sugar to ⅔ cup (120 g). Swap in 2 tablespoons of cornstarch for the flour. Replace the cinnamon and nutmeg with 2 teaspoons of vanilla extract.

INDIVIDUAL CRUMBLES

What could be better than having a sweet little dessert all to yourself? Instead of a large baking dish, divide the filling between eight 8-ounce (225-g) ramekins (or half-pint jars) placed on a rimmed cookie sheet. Divide the topping in the same fashion. Bake for about 40 minutes, until browned and bubbly.

FREEZE IT: If you opt for half-pint jars, you can screw on the lids and freeze these little beauties, unbaked, for up to a few months, then uncover and put them all—or just one—into the oven or toaster oven when you need a little treat. Add a few minutes of baking time when baking from frozen. This version works with the original recipe and both flavor variations.

RHUBARB

For many fans of farmers' markets, the annual arrival of rhubarb signals a delicious new realm of possibilities. Rhubarb inspires childhood memories of harvesting stalks from the garden and dipping them in sugar to cut their bracing tartness. Though it can be used in savory dishes, rhubarb is most often incorporated into baked goods and desserts—a grown-up version of dipping in sugar. It's low in calories and high in vitamins A, B, and K, fiber, and antioxidants. One thing to watch: The leaves are toxic, so if you grow rhubarb or purchase it with leaves still attached, be sure to remove them before heading into the kitchen.

MULTISEED AND QUINOA BREAD

MAKES	1 large loaf
PREP	1 hour 10 minutes
COOK	45 minutes

YOU WILL NEED

1 cup (180 g) cooked quinoa

3 ¾ cups (450 g) strong, white bread flour, plus extra for kneading

¾ cup (75 g) oats

1 tablespoon sunflower seeds

1 tablespoon chia seeds

1 tablespoon flaxseed

1 teaspoon sea salt

1 package (¼ oz./7 g) instant yeast

¼ cup (60 ml) milk

¾ cup (180 ml) warm water

3 tablespoons olive oil

3 tablespoons honey

THIS HEALTHY QUINOA BREAD IS PACKED WITH ASSORTED SEEDS THAT GIVE IT A WONDERFULLY NUTTY TASTE AND TEXTURE. IT MAKES GREAT SANDWICHES AND IS FABULOUS TOASTED, TOO.

1 Put the cooked and cooled quinoa in a large mixing bowl and add the bread flour, oats, mixed seeds, and the sea salt. Mix, and make a well in the center of the ingredients.

2 Add the yeast to the mixture and pour the milk and warm water into the well—mix the liquids in, then add the olive oil and honey, and mix well again with your hands.

3 Turn the dough out onto a floured board and knead for 10 minutes until smooth and elastic. (You can use a food mixer with a dough hook to knead the dough if you wish.)

4 Put the dough in a bowl, cover, and let rise in a warm spot until doubled in size (about 1 hour).

5 Turn the dough out onto a floured board, knock it back, knead again, and then shape it to fit in a well-greased 2-pound (900-g) loaf pan. Let rise once more until doubled in size, about 45 minutes.

6 Preheat the oven to 400°F/200°C/Gas Mark 6, and place a bowl of water in the bottom of the oven.

7 Bake the bread for 35–45 minutes; the bread is cooked when it is crusty, golden brown, and sounds hollow when tapped underneath.

8 Let the bread cool for 15 minutes in the loaf pan before turning it out onto a wire cooling rack. Slice for serving. The bread can be used for sandwiches, toast, grilled cheese, or simply buttered.

RECIPE LIST BY BLOGGER

Karen S. Burns-Booth

Pecan Quinoa Porridge 28

Quinoa, Feta Cheese, and Spinach Breakfast Muffins 44

Smoky Eggplant and Quinoa Dip 58

Quinoa-Coated Fish Stick Sandwich 74

Quinoa Crab Cakes 78

Quinoa Pizza with Blue Cheese and Eggplant 82

Quinoa Couscous with Blood Oranges and Burrata 122

Fluffy and Fruity Quinoa Scones 142

Frosted Orange, Semolina, and Quinoa Cake 164

Multiseed and Quinoa Bread 170

Carolyn Cope

Vanilla Cardamom Quinoa Granola 32

Quinoa Pancakes with Spiced Strawberry Compote
   and Yogurt 36

Quinoa, Cheddar, and Chive Mini Frittatas 48

Vegetable Paella-Style Quinoa 98

Black Bean, Quinoa, and Vegetable Chili 104

Risotto-Style Quinoa with Caramelized Onions
   and Mushrooms 106

Beet and Carrot Quinoa Cakes with
   Cumin Yogurt Sauce 134

Roasted Winter Vegetable, Quinoa, and
   Wild Rice Salad 138

Rich and Fudgy Quinoa Brownies 152

Apple Crisp with Quinoa Crumble Topping 166

Jassy Davis

Quinoa Crêpes with Berries and Ricotta 38

Puffed Quinoa Bhelpuri 66

Sweet Potato Quinoa Kibbeh 68

Sprouted Quinoa Chirashi Sushi Bowl 86

Sprouted Quinoa and Salmon Temaki Sushi 89

Smoky Spanish Quinoa with Chicken and Chorizo 110

Lamb and Quinoa Meatballs 112

Quinoa Kisir with Pomegranate and Walnuts 126

Fruity Quinoa Tabbouleh with Feta Cheese 130

Thai-Style Crab, Pomelo & Quinoa Salad 136

Kristina Sloggett

Toasted Coconut and Quinoa Breakfast Pudding 24

Pumped-Up Five-Layer Quinoa Dip 60

Cheesy Buffalo Quinoa Tots 62

Quinoa Bean Burger with Basil Aioli 92

Spicy Peanut Veggie Stew with Quinoa Dumplings 96

Chipotle Sweet Potato Quinoa Enchiladas 102

Summer Quinoa Salad with Grapefruit Tahini Dressing 128

Power Boost Snickerdoodles 146

Chocolate Peanut Butter Candy Bars 148

Quinoa Cinnamon Power Bites 154

Jackie Sobon

Cacao Quinoa Protein Shake 22

Quinoa Waffles with Berry Compote 40

Quinoa Chickpea Scramble Burrito 51

Quinoa-Dusted Tortilla Chips with Artichoke Arugula
   Dip 56

Southwestern Quinoa Lettuce Cups 70

Veggie and Quinoa Summer Rolls with
   Cajun Tahini Sauce 76

Roasted Cauliflower Quinoa Soup 118

Curry Squash Quinoa Bisque with Coconut Cream 120

Blueberry Pistachio Quinoa Parfait with
   Quinoa Praline 158

Spiced Cashew "Cheesecake" with Red Quinoa Crust 162

ACKNOWLEDGMENTS

Thank you so much to Carolyn Cope who wrote the fantastic introduction to quinoa (pages 10-19).

Thanks to Abi Waters, Anna Southgate, Rachel Malig and Ann Barrett.

Quantum Books would like to thank the following for supplying images for inclusion in this book:
Shutterstock.com: Iryna Melnyk 8-9, Letterberry 10, Elena Shashkina 11, withGod 12, Anna Hoychuk 18, matka_Wariatka 27, Es75 31, Sea Wave 35, sematadesign 43, Evgeny Karandaev 47, D and J foodstyling 65, Olha Afanasieva 73, Jozef Sowa 85, Piyato 91, sarsmis 95, elena moiseeva 101, Maryna Pleshkun 114, Jiri Hera 125, Vasileios Karafillidis 133, bitt24 145, Magdalena Paluchowska 151, Juan Ci 157, Nickola_Che 160, Olha Afanasieva 169.

While every effort has been made to credit contributors, Quantum Books would like to apologize should there have been any omissions or errors and would be pleased to make the appropriate correction to future editions of the book.